Disaster Management Programs for Historic Sites

edited by

Dirk H. R. Spennemann

and

David W. Look

U.S. NATIONAL PARK SERVICE
SAN FRANCISCO, CALIFORNIA, U.S.A.

—

WESTERN CHAPTER OF THE ASSOCIATION
FOR PRESERVATION TECHNOLOGY
SAN FRANCISCO, CALIFORNIA, U.S.A.

—

THE JOHNSTONE CENTRE, CHARLES STURT UNIVERSITY
ALBURY, AUSTRALIA

1998

Disaster Management Programs for Historic Sites/ edited by Dirk H.R. Spennemann
and David W. Look.
p.cm.
Proceedings of a symposium organized by the U.S. National Park Service, Western
Regional Office, San Francisco, incollaboration with the Western Chapter of the
Association for Preservation Technology, and held June 27-29, 1997 in San Francisco.
Includes bibliogrpahical references and index.
ISBN 1-893076-00-8 (alk. paper)
1. Historic sites -- United States--Management--Congresses. 2. Emergency management--
United States--Congresses. 3. Disasters--United States--Congresses. 4. Cultural property--
Protection--United States--Congresses. I. Spennemann, Dirk. R. II. Look, David W. III.
United States. National Park Service, Western Regional Office. IV. Association for
Preservation Technology. Western Chapter. V. Johnstone Centre of Parks, Recreation,
and Heritage.
E159.D57 1998
363.6'9'0973--dc21   98-40705
                                                                                          CIP

This symposium was made possible, in part, with special funding by the U.S. National Park
Service through its Cultural Resources Training Initiative. However, the contents and opinions
expressed in this publication do not necessarily reflect the views or policies of the National Park
Service, U.S. Department of the Interior, United States of America; Johnstone Centre for Parks,
Recreation, and Heritage, Charles Sturt Unversity; or the Western Chapter of the Association for
Preservation Technology, who partially funded the production.

Regulations of the U.S. Department of the Interior strictly prohibit unlawful discrimination in
departmental Federally Assisted programs on the basis of race, color, national origin, age, sex,
sexual orientation, or handicap. Any person who believes he or she has been discriminated
against in any program, activity, or facility operated by a recipient of Federal assistance should
write to: Director, Equal Opportunity Program, U.S. Department of the Interior, National Park
Service, P.O. Box 37127, Washington, DC 20013-7127, U.S.A.

This document is printed on acid free archival bond paper.

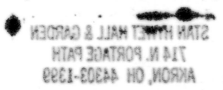

Spennemann, Dirk H. R. & David W. Look (1998)
'Preface', in *Disaster Management Programs for Historic Sites*, eds Dirk H. R. Spennemann & David W. Look. San Francisco and Albury: Association for Preservation Technology (Western Chapter) and The Johnstone Centre, Charles Sturt University. Pp. iii-v.

Preface

DIRK H. R. SPENNEMANN [¶]
DAVID W. LOOK [†]

The United Nations designated the 1990s as the Decade for Natural Hazard Reduction. It is ironic that natural disasters are an increasingly common occurrence in the 1990s, both due to random chance and, as far as the meteorological hazards are concerned, due to climatic changes. Natural phenomena are considered disasters only when they adversely affect lives and property. For example, an earthquake or flood in a sparsely populated part of the United States is seldom declared a disaster. The number and magnitude of disasters seems to be increasing. Humans cannot control or significantly change the forces of nature. However, there are steps that can be taken to lessen or mitigate the effects of natural phenomena and/or better prepare to cope with the damage of the disasters when they happen. Although human behavior is about as difficult to control as nature, there are also steps that can be taken to prevent man-made disasters and to limit the damage caused by them. What can be done?

In many of the recent events, vast sections of the cultural heritage were impaired, largely by the direct impact of the disasters, but also, and by no small measure, by the actions taken by the hazard mitigation and response teams. As the safeguarding of life and property takes precedence, any other consideration plays a minor role in the disaster response phase. In many cases, damaged historic places are deemed to be a safety hazard and are ordered to be demolished by building officials without due consideration being given to (a) their cultural heritage value and (b) the possibility of their being stabilized and restored. Thus, potential for conflict abounds and, historically, conflict has ensued between the various management agencies. This has been the case in the United States, as well as in Australia.

There was a need to bring together the two different sides of the equation - the disaster management authorities on the one hand and the cultural resource managers on the other -

---

[¶] The Johnstone Centre, Charles Sturt University, PO Box 789, Albury NSW 2640, Australia.
E-mail: dspennemann@csu.edu.au
[†] US National Park Service, Western Regional Office, 600 Harrison Street, San Francisco, CA 94104-1372, USA.
E-mail: david_w_look@nps.gov

and to establish a dialogue which would facilitate future protection of heritage items. In 1995 we were half-way through the United Nations Decade for Natural Hazard Reduction. We had to ask questions such as: What has worked well? What has not worked? What can be improved? How can we best share what we have learned before we forget it?

To this end, a symposium was organized by the US National Park Service (Western Regional Office, San Francisco) in collaboration with the Western Chapter of the Association for Preservation Technology. The symposium *Management of disaster mitigation and response programs for historic sites: a dialogue*, held from 27-29 June in San Francisco, saw participants from throughout the United States with a sprinkling of foreigners from Palau, the Marshall Islands and Australia. The symposium focused on the US management systems and US experiences, but many aspects have relevance well beyond North America. The symposium was limited to about sixty people to maximize the exchange of ideas and opinions and to stimulate discussion. Some forty people presented papers or discussion platforms.

The three-day symposium was marked by a general climate of cooperation and a preparedness by all speakers to exert a concerted effort for communication and mutual understanding of the other's point of view. Even though initially no publication had been planned, it was deemed important to make some of the information available to non-participants. The production of the volume was delayed for numerous reasons, not least the dearth of funding available to produce the volume.

The volume presented here is obviously only the first step in a progression of research and practical work. The publication of these papers will hopefully spawn more research and further conferences to exchange ideas, approaches and strategies.

In publishing these proceedings, we are aware of the poignancy of a joke told by Blaine Cliver during one of the sessions:

> This is a short little disaster story about the man who had survived the Johnstown (Pennsylvania) Flood (of the late 19th century). It had been a horrifying experience for the man and afterwards, he found that he had to go up to almost everyone he saw and grab them by their arm and say, "I have to tell you what happened to me in the Johnstown Flood." This went on for the rest of his life. Eventually, the man finally died and went to heaven. As he came to the Pearly Gates of Heaven, the man was met by St. Peter who greeted him saying, "Welcome! What can I do for you?" The man responded to St. Peter by saying that he had this great problem in that he has to tell everyone he ever met about his horrible experience in the Johnstown Flood. The man asked St. Peter if it would be possible to gather everyone in heaven together so that the man could tell his story only once and then it would be all over for him. St. Peter said that would be difficult, but that he would look into it. St Peter then talked to David Look's counterpart who arranged meetings in heaven and everything was set. The next day, when St. Peter saw the man again, St. Peter told him, "Be here at 8:30 tomorrow morning and you can tell your story." The man was overjoyed and thanked St. Peter profusely. As they parted, St. Peter said to the man, "I must warn you that Noah has asked to say a few words after you speak."

Let Noah come forward!

Acknowledgments

The organization of the symposium was made possible through the assistance of Glenn Matthews (APT). The Western Chapter of the Association for Preservation Technology also made available funds that permitted this book to be published.

The editors are indebted to those speakers of the conference who provided manuscripts and illustrations for inclusion in this volume. Illustrations were made available by Daryl Barksdale, Steade Craigo, Alex Kimmelman, Daniel Shapiro, Dirk Spennemann, and Thomas Winter.

George Siekkinen transcribed the papers presented at the panel that he chaired. his work is gratefully acknowledged.

Pam Milliken (The Johnstone Centre, Charles Sturt University) copy-edited the papers in this volume.

Contents

Spennemann, Dirk H. R. & David W. Look (1998)
'Managing disasters and managing disaster responses:
an introduction', in *Disaster Management Programs for
Historic Sites*, eds Dirk H. R. Spennemann & David W.
Look. San Francisco and Albury: Association for
Preservation Technology (Western Chapter) and The
Johnstone Centre, Charles Sturt University. Pp. 1-5.

Managing disasters and managing disaster responses: an introduction

DIRK H. R. SPENNEMANN [¶]
DAVID W. LOOK [†]

Over the last several years, the United States has experienced an unprecedented series of disasters: earthquakes; hurricanes; typhoons; tornadoes; floods; landslides; oil spills and accidents involving other toxic substances; fires; civil disturbances; and terrorist attacks. Most of these have destroyed or severely damaged archaeological and historic sites including cultural landscapes.

Heritage conservation and disaster management in the United States are two fields that depend on a working relationship at the federal, state and local levels. They are both good examples of partnerships in government, but the two fields have not always interacted effectively. What are the respective responsibilities, roles and functions? As federal, state and local governments downsize, there will be fewer cultural resource management staff to respond to future disasters. How can we be more effective and efficient? There was a certainly a need to look at a number of agreements developed after various disasters and at a proposal for an 'umbrella' agreement developed by the Advisory Council on Historic Preservation and the Federal Emergency Management Agency (FEMA). The umbrella agreement would be in place before future disasters and amended for each disaster.

The contributions to this volume can be grouped under six major headings:

- Intergovernmental cooperation on the national and local level;

[¶] The Johnstone Centre, Charles Sturt University, PO Box 789, Albury NSW 2640, Australia.
E-mail: dspennemann@csu.edu.au
[†] US National Park Service, Western Regional Office, 600 Harrison Street, San Francisco, CA 94104-1372, USA.
E-mail: david_w_look@nps.gov

- The recognition of significant historic character and fabric in a post-disaster situation;

- Seismic safety and rehabilitation;

- Floods and cyclones;

- Terrorist Attack;

- Communication and training.

Intergovernmental cooperation at the national, state and local level

The effects of natural disasters transcend the boundaries of responsibilities of any federal government agency. Too often in the past, the various agencies were in disagreement on how to proceed, and the resulting tension often lingered well after the disaster and its aftermath had been overcome. Clearly, cooperation was needed.

Memoranda of agreement and programmatic agreements among the key players of disaster mitigation and historic preservation have been in place since 1993. How the Advisory Council on Historic Preservation, the Federal Emergency Management Agency (FEMA), the National Park Service and other federal and state agencies can cooperate and assist in future disasters is explored by a number of papers drawing on past experiences in California, the Midwest and Washington State. The key component of a successful programmatic agreement is that both sides stand to benefit.

Lisa Katchka traces the development of programmatic agreements from a FEMA perspective. Following the 1993 Midwest Floods, which affected several states, regional cooperation and standardized approaches were required. Programmatic agreements allowed federal agencies, such as FEMA, to use a *uniform* process for all states signing that agreement to facilitate rapid responses. Some instances were deemed outside the umbrella of the programmatic agreement, resulting in individual memoranda of agreement.

Cherilyn Widell outlines a Memorandum of Agreement between the California State Historic Preservation Office (SHPO) and FEMA signed two weeks after the Northridge Earthquake of 17 January 1994. It governed the actions of the Section 106 process. The programmatic agreement allowed SHPO staff to draw on technical and engineering expertise which was unavailable in-house and which allowed rapid assessment of National Register eligible structures.

The interplay of state and local governments and the historic preservation community following the Loma Prieta (1989) and Northridge (1994) events is chronicled and critically addressed by *Steade Craigo*. In the days following Loma Prieta, many historic properties were demolished with little, if any, input from the preservation community.

As *Wayne Donaldson* points out, the vast majority of crucial decisions on the future of damaged historic properties are made in the first ten days following the disaster event. He advanced a number of issues that should be taken into account to mitigate the impact of disaster managers.

The last two papers in this section look at more practical aspects of pre- and post-disaster management. *Alex Kimmelman* discusses practicalities of disaster planning and hazard mitigation of identification of historic sites; distribution and archiving of studies and resources; and the processes of selecting suitable contractors. He also highlights the opportunities presented by damaged structures to assess and document their method of construction.

Jorge Alfaro considers the issue of funding the disaster recovery programs. He argues that local communities need to take the lead in the funding programs and use federal funds to augment the required funding. He exemplifies this with the success of San Francisco's bond programs and the seismic retrofit and rehabilitation that could be funded through these opportunities.

The recognition of significant historic character and fabric in a post-disaster situation

A common thread through many accounts of post-disaster situations is the comment that the historic fabric of a building was not been recognized as being of appropriate cultural value. As a result, the structure was pulled down.

George Siekkinen addresses the ethical issues and argues that any loss of historic fabric is deplorable as it diminishes the integrity of the building. He points to the conceptual schism in the minds of many administrators who happily apply different standards of integrity to items of moveable cultural heritage on the one hand, and buildings on the other.

Good documentation of the existing structure and fabric, and detailed disaster preparedness planning can minimize the impact of a disaster event on cultural properties. *Blaine Cliver* demonstrates this well in the case example of the Franklin Delano Roosevelt Mansion.

Wayne Donaldson makes the comment that several historic buildings have been exceptionally well designed, but that the lack of knowledge about the nature and capabilities of the designs has led to the demolition of many buildings which were only slightly damaged. He demonstrates the variability in building design in California and argues for a systematic and detailed assessment of historic building practices.

Commonly damaged buildings are pulled down following a disaster event regardless of whether the building is worth saving from a conservation point of view and regardless of the feasibility of such action. *John Kariotis* highlights the fact that the reasons of 'life safety' so often put forward as arguments for demolitions rarely warrant demolition. He presents a number of cases where the acceptable risk of earthquake-related injury posed by historic buildings is very low, even though the structure may sustain (repairable) damage.

Seismic safety and rehabilitation

Given that the conference was held in San Francisco, it is not surprising that the majority of the papers dealt with earthquakes and seismic retrofit rather than other forms of disasters.

When is seismic rehabilitation required? *Diana Todd* outlines the work by the Interagency Committee on Seismic Safety in Construction which develops standards for federally owned or leased buildings. She specifies activities which automatically trigger a seismic (re-)evaluation. Essentially, each fundamental change in a building's use or modification can act as a trigger.

Private sector buildings are considered by *Ugo Morelli*. The development of the seismic retrofit standards developed by FEMA are described in his paper.

Robert Mackensen discusses the California State Historical Building Code and its application to pre- and post-disaster situations. He argues that some of the seismic retrofit work required after an earthquake event may be prohibitively expensive, leaving an owner little choice but to take up the offer to have the damaged building demolished for free. The California Building Code essentially allows the reconstruction of a building with little modification as long as basic safety standards are met.

Randolph Langenbach addresses a number of practical and ethical issues in seismic retrofit, illustrating the need for structure specific investigations lest the unique historic records of each building be lost accidentally. His paper critically evaluates the current design standards and questions their applicability to historic structures. Gutting of structures and a radical redesigning of the internal layout following seismic retrofit are only too common.

While *Daniel Shapiro* provides some background on national guidelines for the seismic rehabilitation of buildings, *Stephen Mathison* addresses the application of the Secretary of the Interior Standards for Rehabilitation to structures affected by disasters.

The final two contributions in this section look at case studies of earthquakes. *Steade Craigo* provides an overview of the past history of earthquake-affected heritage properties in California. *Thomas Winter* describes the impact of the 1994 Northridge earthquake on a structure in Los Encinos State Historic Park and the restoration and seismic retrofit work required.

Floods and cyclones

Circular high speed wind systems (cyclones/typhoons/hurricanes, tropical storms and tornadoes) wreak havoc on historic and archaeological sites. The associated rain causes flooding of low-lying places and urban areas.

Dirk Spennemann discusses the effects of cyclones on archaeological sites in Australia and the Pacific and discusses the management options available. His paper demonstrates the destructive forces of cyclones on coastal sites and shows that there are no protection options available given the number and spread of the sites.

Daryl Barksdale describes the impact of Tropical Storm Alberto on Georgia. The storm, a 500-year event, caught the Historic Preservation Office by surprise. Barksdale describes the recovery experiences and shows that, because of the rural setting, only few sites had been assessed prior to the flooding event.

In the final paper in this section, *Alice Baldrica* addresses the problems caused by sheet flooding of archaeological sites. Following continued rains, the internal overflow lakes of the Humboldt and Carson Rivers were full and threatened communities with flooding. A natural dyke between the two basins was artificially beached to reduce flooding. Wind and wave action in the shallow lakes which formed had stripped the sediment cover from several archaeological sites causing their exposure and subsequent erosion. As with the case of the tropical cyclones, the number of sites affected was such that salvage excavation was deemed impractical.

Terrorist Attack

Urban unrest and terrorist attack not only exact human casualties and often deaths, but the accompanying destruction of property also causes damage to historic structures. The attack on the Uffici in Florence in 1993 is a prime example where cultural institutions became the prime target. To highlight the increasing importance of the issue we have dedicated a separate section to the single paper addressing the issue.

Eva Osborne describes the aftermath of the terrorist bombing of the Alfred P. Murrah Federal Building, Oklahoma City, on 19 April 1995. The bombing caught the historic preservation community, as well as the rest of the population, completely unprepared. The physical effects of the bomb blast on the structures were complex, as they combined a number of forces. The blast air wave caused effects similar to tornadoes, while the underground shock wave caused damage similar to those by severe earthquakes of very short duration.

Communication and training

The final section touches upon issues of training and communications. In his paper, *Dirk Spennemann* argues the case for an integrated training course on historic heritage management in disaster and post-disaster context. *Dirk Spennemann* and *David Green* describe a model for a information network based on the World Wide Web. Both papers stress the need for communication to overcome the shortcomings of current problems.

The final chapter is a summation of the key issues by the editors with a suggestion of the directions we may need to take to ensure the survival of our historic buildings in future disaster events. Clearly, these papers are only a first step, but a necessary one.

INTERGOVERNMENTAL COOPERATION AT THE NATIONAL AND LOCAL LEVEL

Katchka, Lisa (1998) 'Memoranda of Agreement and
Programmatic Agreements in the disaster context', in
Disaster Management Programs for Historic Sites, eds
Dirk H. R. Spennemann & David W. Look. San
Francisco and Albury: Association for Preservation
Technology (Western Chapter) and The Johnstone
Centre, Charles Sturt University. Pp. 9-12.

1

Memoranda of Agreement and Programmatic Agreements in the disaster context

LISA KATCHKA [¶]

As two of the Federal Emergency Management Agency's main program objectives include recovery efforts for victims of a disaster, it is important that Federal Emergency Management Agency (FEMA) actions be allowed to proceed in as timely a manner as possible. With respect to fulfilling our responsibilities under Section 106 of the National Historic Preservation Act, FEMA's Historic Preservation Officer has worked closely with the Advisory Council on Historic Preservation to streamline the standard review process.

Programmatic Agreements

The programmatic agreement allows for the requirements of the National Historic Preservation Act to be carried out in a manner tailored to the program requirements, time line and resources of FEMA. There are a number of ways in which the programmatic agreement has simplified the Section 106 review process:

1. Firstly, at the earliest moments of disaster response, the programmatic agreement assigns various responsibilities of historic preservation review to certain agencies or entities:
   - the programmatic agreement establishes partnerships among FEMA, the State, the State Historic Preservation Officer (SHPO) and the Advisory Council on Historic Preservation; and

[¶] Office of General Counsel, Federal Emergency Management Agency, 500 C Street, SW, Room 840, Washington, DC 20472, USA

- the programmatic agreement delegates responsibilities to the SHPO to assure that effects on historic and archaeological resources are considered; and delays to FEMA's delivery of assistance will be minimal. The programmatic agreement also can provide for a mechanism of reimbursement to SHPO for identification, evaluation and review activities not required of the SHPO under the standard Section 106 review process.

2. Secondly, the programmatic agreement spells out specific procedures which short cut the process otherwise outlined in Part 800:

   - excludes from SHPO and the Advisory Council on Historic Preservation review routine activities with little potential to adversely affect historic properties (plumbing and electrical modifications, etc.);

   - abbreviates the time frames for SHPO and Council reviews still required by the programmatic agreement; and

   - provides standard treatment measures for adverse effects.

First Midwest Floods Programmatic Agreement

The first programmatic agreement which was fully coordinated between FEMA and the Advisory Council on Historic Preservation to address historic preservation efforts was developed in the aftermath of the 1993 Midwest Floods. The 1993 Floods were particularly suited to the programmatic agreement concept, since the floods had affected a large area across a number of states, resulting in similar damages to homes and public buildings.

- To address all of these projects, essentially simultaneously, through the full Section 106 process, would have taxed FEMA resources beyond our capabilities; the programmatic agreement simplified the process greatly, reducing the steps and obligations required by FEMA;

- The programmatic agreement also provided a means to assure a somewhat standardized process by which all of the midwestern states would handle historic review, as the identical agreement was used in each state; and

- The process of developing the programmatic agreement provided an opportunity for the Advisory Council on Historic Preservation and FEMA to make the Regional offices, the States and even the SHPOs more aware of the requirements of the National Historic Preservation Act and their respective roles in conducting historic review.

Since then, the programmatic agreement used for the Midwest agreements has gone through a number of changes and become more refined with each subsequent agreement -

used in Georgia, Texas and in California for both the earthquakes and the flooding here in the north.

Nationwide Programmatic Agreement

The concept of the programmatic agreement continues to evolve with each draft that is developed for a new disaster. As FEMA has responded to more types of disasters with programmatic agreements, has encountered a greater variety of historic and cultural resources to be covered by the agreements (historic churches or city halls damaged by flood or earthquake, petroglyphs on quarry walls from which stone may be taken for a FEMA action, archaeological artifacts or Indian burial grounds at project sites), and as we have grown familiar with the types of FEMA activities which are *not* likely to adversely affect such resources, the programmatic agreement has evolved into a more comprehensive document.

Consequently, FEMA has initiated a project to develop a 'Nationwide Programmatic Agreement' which would act as an umbrella agreement which would apply to any disaster occurring anywhere in the country, and would further expedite FEMA's ability to react quickly in initiating disaster recovery and mitigation projects, as FEMA and the Advisory Council on Historic Preservation would not have to negotiate a new programmatic agreement each time there was a disaster. The development of the Nationwide programmatic agreement is an ideal opportunity to coordinate with the Council, other agencies and the states to arrive at a thoughtful and workable document, based on the input of a range of experiences and interests. This agreement, currently in draft form, will be circulated to the states through the National Emergency Management Association and to the SHPOs through the National Conference of State Historic Preservation Officers.

Memoranda of Agreements

The last issue I want to touch on are the memoranda of agreement. Although a programmatic agreement is intended to cover the bulk of all projects which are likely to arise in the course of disaster recovery or mitigation efforts with respect to any given disaster, there are sometimes projects arising from a disaster not covered by a programmatic agreement, or projects which are so large in scope and potential adverse effect that the increased surveying, review, consultation, treatment, documentation or controversy warrants a special agreement to address just the procedures for fulfilling Section 106 requirements for that project.

Whereas the key to an effective programmatic agreement seems to be to anticipate the issues which may arise in order to provide for treatment and coordination which will speed the Section 106 process along, the key to an effective memoranda of agreement seems to be the pre-agreement coordination of the Agency with interested parties.

There are several examples of where historic preservation groups provided input into the memoranda of agreement process with respect to a number of historic structures in California, such as San Francisco City Hall of the Los Angeles Coliseum. Probably the ultimate example of public participation from the FEMA experience was the proposal to rebuild a marine laboratory at a new site happened to contain a number of archaeological resources including - for example, Native American artifacts, midden, lithic workshop and remnants of human remains suggesting a possible Native American burial ground. In this case, an interest group sprang up to oppose the project and, of course, there were Native American interests to be considered. The result was a very lengthy memoranda of agreement process, which it seemed would not end even when the signatures were collected, and that entailed more than giving the interested parties a chance to review the draft memoranda of agreement. It was not even clear who was entitled to be an interested party, as individual claims of tribal descent were not coming just from individuals recognized officially by the United States to be legal descendants.

The memoranda of agreement eventually included a number of innovative ways of retaining the Native American input throughout the project implementation, involving them in plan review, treatment and data recovery review, etc. In addition, the applicant agreed to implement an educational exhibit dealing with Native American culture, lifestyles and archaeology in cooperation with the Native Americans concurring in the memoranda of agreement. With the cooperation of the California SHPO and the Advisory Council on Historic Preservation, the memoranda of agreement seems now to have had a happy ending.

Conclusion

By way of conclusion, I would like to point out that through all of the agreements - programmatic agreements or memoranda of agreements - the Advisory Council on Historic Preservation, the SHPOs, the State Emergency offices and FEMA coordinated throughout on process and shared responsibilities, as well as on determining the language to be used to reflect those agreements. I expect that the same coordination will result in a useful nationwide programmatic agreement in the coming months.

Widell, Cherilyn (1998) 'The government's respon-
sibilities for the preservation of cultural resources', in
Disaster Management Programs for Historic Sites, eds
Dirk H. R. Spennemann & David W. Look. San
Francisco and Albury: Association for Preservation
Technology (Western Chapter) and The Johnstone
Centre, Charles Sturt University. Pp. 13-15.

2

The government's responsibilities for the preservation of cultural resources

CHERILYN WIDELL [¶]

Despite local preservation ordinances since the 1930s, state landmarks' programs and the National Historic Preservation Act of 1966, there continues to be a black hole of understanding at all levels of government and with the public about what it means to be designated a historical property. In the best of circumstances, it is extremely difficult to walk into a town, announce that a property is eligible for the National Register of Historic Places and if you are planning to use federal money, you will need to go through state and federal review.

In time of emergency when our human instinct is crying to gain control, to strike back and show strength, demolition nicely fills those needs. Woe to that person that says "No! Wait, shore it up, this property is historic, there might be money because your property is historic; you do not have to tear it down right away. Let us help you find a solution."

The role of assessing historic sites after the 1994 Northridge Earthquake fell to the State Historic Preservation Officer (SHPO) through a SHPO representative and through a new and very innovative Programmatic Agreement among the Federal Emergency Management Agency (FEMA), the California Office of Emergency Services, the Advisory Council on Historic Preservation and SHPO. Signed on 1 February 1994 by then Acting SHPO,

---

[¶] State Historic Preservation Officer, California State Office of Historic Preservation, California Department of Parks & Recreation, PO Box 942896, Sacramento, CA 94296-0001, USA

Steade Craigo (two days before my appointment as SHPO), I cannot take credit for the innovations in the document which was mostly developed with FEMA by Hans Kreutzberg of the California SHPO and Lee Keatinge of the Advisory Council on Historic Preservation.

Among the innovations were the assumption of normal Federal Agency responsibility of assessing areas of potential effects, determination of eligibility for listing in the National Register of Historic Places, and Section 106 review of project effects, all to be conducted by the SHPO through a SHPO Representative to be paid by FEMA.

The contractor selected - prior to my appointment was the Historic Resources Group - Christy McAvoy and Bill Delvac, principals - located right in the middle of the affected area in Hollywood.

Some responsibilities in addition to the normal Section 106 process were:

- Staff the FEMA Disaster Field Office;

- Provide five-day turnaround times on determination of eligibility for listings and effects;

- Help in developing a large electronic data base of historic properties;

- Standard mitigation.

Final decision-making and appeal always remained with the SHPO.

This programmatic agreement worked; it worked very, very well. Through it we were able to:

- Provide knowledgeable individuals in a timely manner on a regular basis at a time when local travel was very tough;

- Tap into local knowledge and political expertise and a network of trust;

- Acquire additional design and engineering expertise unavailable from SHPO;

- Provide 24-hour service to National Historic Landmark Los Angeles Coliseum.

We reviewed 1,700 historic buildings; about 600 were eligible for the National Register of Historic Places. This programmatic agreement will be used again for California floods and is used as a model throughout the United States by FEMA.

Coordinating federal, state and local government levels of activity

Earlier earthquakes were followed by difficult and strained coordination among the various levels of government. Now, with the programmatic agreement in hand, federal and state levels are working together in a coordinated effort. It is import to build support ahead of time (before the disaster strikes). The key area to concentrate now is at the local level to build trust and understanding *outside* the preservation community.

After a disaster strikes, the first response is by the building officials of California who use the Applied Technology Council - 20 to placard buildings:

- Red: hazardous, do not enter;

- Yellow: may be hazardous, do not enter until there is a further assessment by a licensed engineer;

- Green: not hazardous, may be entered.

The rapid assessment conducted by the building officers in twenty minutes is not an in-depth engineering study. Consequently, a red tag does not mean that the building must be demolished. Unfortunately, the mass media misinterprets a red tag to mean demolition.

A damaged historic building may only be hazardous until it has been secured and stabilized. Shoring Standards are needed. Roy Harthorn, a Santa Barbara Building Official, is working on Shoring Standards for Damaged Buildings. We need more training through the Safety/Emergency Committee of California Building Officials and more use of shoring as an initial remedy to give time for full assessment and consideration. We also need more use of on-line assessment capability through powerbooks (portable computers) and we have initiated discussion with the Office of Emergency Services.

Finally, and most importantly, we must use current assessment surveys to target mitigation against seismic activity in the future. California Senate Bill 875 would provide tax credits for seismic retrofit. We need more education on mitigating hazards rather than more regulations. Seismic retrofit will not only save lives, but it will also help to preserve our irreplaceable cultural resources.

Craigo, Steade (1998) 'A helping hand', in *Disaster Management Programs for Historic Sites*, eds Dirk H. R. Spennemann & David W. Look. San Francisco and Albury: Association for Preservation Technology (Western Chapter) and The Johnstone Centre, Charles Sturt University. Pp. 17-24.

3

A helping hand

STEADE CRAIGO [¶]

There is a saying that goes something like "I am from the government and I am here to help you". Help is what historic preservationists wanted to provide during recent California disasters, but we soon discovered that providing assistance is not easy, nor always appreciated.

Unlike other states, California has been spared from disasters such as the horrible Hurricane Andrew that struck Louisiana, the widespread floods of the midwest, the terrible oil spill in Alaska, and disastrous Hurricane Iniki that struck Hawaii, and the horrendous Oklahoma City terrorist bombing.

Recently, the 'Golden State' has had a variety of disasters, including fires, oil spills, drought, floods, civil disturbances and earthquakes. These disasters have shared similar aspects: the wrecking of the infrastructure, damaged buildings, the economy decimated, thousands of people homeless, and damaged or destroyed historic sites. By far, earthquakes are California's most devastating disaster, and have been a painful lesson for the state and the preservation community.

Californians' written earthquake history goes back to the 18th century; many of the early mission settlements sent accounts to Spain and Mexico often including reports of earthquake damage to their adobe and stone structures and of the rebuilding efforts by the Mission fathers and the Native Californians. The 19th and 20th centuries also had their share of earthquakes. The 1906 San Francisco Earthquake and Fire is one of the more horrible disasters.

Given this well known and documented history of disaster, the 1989 Loma Prieta Earthquake nevertheless took the California preservation community and many municipal

---

[¶] Historical Architect California Office of Historic Preservation, California Department of Parks and Recreation, PO Box 942896, Sacramento, CA 94296-0001, USA. E-mail: calshpo@quiknet.com

governments by surprise. Large urban centers, such as San Francisco and Oakland, responded well to the disaster, but most hard-struck, smaller cities and towns were caught unprepared.

Many unreinforced masonry buildings, mostly in central downtowns, were lost. Over 472 historic buildings were damaged and 78 demolished. The business districts in the towns of Watsonville and Santa Cruz have been considerably and permanently altered by the event.

In one case, the Pacific Garden Historic District in Santa Cruz, the centerpiece of the City's downtown revitalization efforts and a major tourist destination, was officially removed from the National Register of Historic Places because 17 of the 36 contributing historic structures were demolished. This was the first time that an entire historic district has been removed from the National Register.

California is always "between earthquakes", to paraphrase one preservationist (Feilden 1987). Although we are not as prepared as we should be, significant changes were made to improve disaster response during the more recent Northridge Earthquake of January 1994. To provide background, I first want to describe typical disaster problems experienced in the 1989 Loma Prieta Earthquake, and then to explain changes implemented in the 1994 Northridge Disaster.

What becomes clear is that none of the regular environmental protections, and property rights exist during the emergency period, and that a disaster provides a golden opportunity for urban renewal.

Immediately after the Loma Prieta Earthquake struck, state and national preservation agencies, including the National Park Service and the National Trust for Historic Preservation, and statewide nonprofit organizations, attempted to help the worst hit smaller cities and towns. The task was impossible. Towns like Watsonville, Salinas, and Hollister had larger problems than worrying about historic buildings. Thousands of people were homeless and the infrastructure destroyed or in ruins.

Demolitions of historic buildings occurred quickly, with or without owner consent. Many owners were not willing to challenge demolition orders. The normal local, state, and federal environmental protection laws and permitting processes were suspended. This included the Section 106 regulation under the National Historic Preservation Act, the review and comment process required when a federally funded undertaking, such as demolition funded by the Federal Emergency Management Agency (FEMA), affects a building on or eligible for the National Register. This situation will exist as long as the emergency period exists.

Inaccurate and incomplete information spread very quickly, especially regarding what the FEMA would fund. This was disastrous to damaged historic buildings. Property owners were told that FEMA would pay for demolition only within thirty days of the disaster. The owners were often not told that FEMA would also pay for shoring, stabilizing or fencing buildings to eliminate imminent threat to adjacent buildings and to life safety.

Since FEMA money cannot be used to repair private properties, one major disaster problem was an almost total lack of funding for privately owned buildings, both commercial and residential, and also sacred structures. Some owners were quick to take advantage of the federal demolition funding rather then use their own, especially where local officials were pushing hard for demolition. Other owners, who did not want to demolish, soon found themselves in a dilemma because they were unable to afford even the low interest loans that are available during a disaster for private commercial and residential properties from the federal Small Business Administration.

Unfortunately, state preservation agencies, like the California Office of Historic Preservation and the State Historical Building Safety Board, which administers the State Historical Building Code, the prevailing code for historic buildings, did not have official roles which would permit working with federal and state emergency agencies and local governments. Preservationists were officially 'outsiders'.

Thus, preservationists had a very difficult time providing professional expertise to government officials. We found ourselves having little, if any, role in the crucial decisions regarding tagging and demolition of historic buildings, and providing property owners with much needed technical advice. However, this situation quickly began to change.

To slow the rush of demolitions, State Senate Bill 3X was signed by the Governor as part of the Special Emergency Legislation for the Loma Prieta Earthquake. This law, now a permanent part of the California Public Resources Code, Section 5028, requires the approval of the state Office of Historic Preservation before demolition of a historic building can occur, unless 'imminent threat' to life safety or adjacent buildings exists. This key imminent threat decision remains in the hands of the local government.

The impact of this new law was only as good as the preservation ethic was strong in the local communities. The town of Los Gatos, a model preservation community, complied with Public Resources Code 5028. Other cities continued demolishing buildings.

A lawsuit was filed by preservationists against the City of Santa Cruz, challenging the City's failure to abide by Public Resources Code 5028, but this was unsuccessful; and the historic St. George Hotel was demolished. A later legislative attempt to provide technical corrections and to strengthen Public Resources Code 5028 also failed.

Public Resources Code 5028 is a vague, confusing law needing technical corrections. The law does not define 'natural disaster', nor tie the event to a Governor's or President's emergency declaration. 'Imminent threat' is also undefined, permitting varying, inconsistent interpretations by local governments.

The long-term impacts of the Loma Prieta Earthquake on California are frightening. As one preservationist accurately predicted, the shock waves of the disaster will continue on for years. Numerous laws have been passed to increase public safety, and existing laws dusted off and enforced with renewed concern. Since most of the buildings damaged by the Loma Prieta Earthquake were constructed of unreinforced masonry, the 1986 State Unreinforced Masonry Law is one of these that was more rigorously enforced after the quake. This law requires local jurisdictions to identify potentially dangerous unreinforced masonry structures and to adopt plans for mitigating hazards.

The Unreinforced Masonry Law does not require owners to retrofit their buildings; local governments are required only to provide surveys and mitigation plans to the State Seismic

Safety Commission. However, local governments decided that the state law created a 'red hot liability issue' and, in turn, passed the liability problem onto property owners.

As a consequence, cities began adopting mandatory seismic retrofit ordinances. Owners of unreinforced masonry buildings are usually given a specific time to complete the structural retrofit; if this is not accomplished, the building can be declared a hazard and abated, forcing tenants out and demolishing the structures.

Seismic retrofit programs were implemented long before the Loma Prieta Earthquake. San Francisco's early parapet abatement program proved its value as a life-saver during the earthquake. Other local jurisdictions, like the City of Los Angeles, required mandatory seismic retrofit requirements for unreinforced masonry structures. The Los Angeles program also protected lives during the Northridge Disaster.

Figure 3.1. Unreinforced masonry apartment building in Hollywood (CA) showing typical earthquake damage at the corner. A completed seismic retrofit would have prevented such heavy damage. Northridge Earthquake 1994. (Photo: Steade Craigo 1994).

Unfortunately, little financial assistance was and is available for property owners to retrofit buildings. This is a point that the Office of Historic Preservation and other preservation organizations have repeatedly made to the Legislature and the Seismic Safety Commission. Ironically, the City of Santa Cruz had a seismic retrofit ordinance for commercial buildings, which was not enforced due to property owners' lack of funds.

Several years after Loma Prieta, an extremely important agreement was reached with the State Office of Emergency Services, which had a major impact on the response to the 1994 Northridge Disaster. This agreement included the Office of Historic Preservation in the State's Administrative Plan for Public Disaster Assistance. The Office of Historic Preservation now has an official relationship with the following a declaration of a major disaster. The State Historical Building Safety Board is also included in the Plan.

The Office of Historic Preservation responsibilities include providing technical assistance and advice to Office of Emergency Services, local governments and property owners regarding the Section 106 process; providing preservation personnel at the Disaster Field Office to expedite review of historic projects; and conducting surveys of potentially eligible historic structures.

Just as importantly, the Office of Historic Preservation and the State Historical Building Safety Board will work with the Office of Emergency Services disaster preparedness activities, including training for state inspectors, employees and public inspectors.

In the Northridge Earthquake, a fundamental response change occurred by providing an Office of Historic Preservation presence at the disaster site to help expedite recovery. In the programmatic agreement between FEMA, National Advisory Council For Historic Preservation, and the State Office of Emergency Services, the California State Historic Preservation Officer (SHPO) delegated SHPO authority under Section 106 to a local representative to identify buildings on or eligible for the National Register and to provide comments on FEMA-funded activities. Only in the case of an adverse impact determination would the review come directly to the SHPO in Sacramento.

Having a SHPO-authorized local representative, with the technical expertise needed at the disaster site immediately after the earthquake first struck, greatly improved communications and significantly expedited emergency response. This arrangement was especially helpful with high visibility projects like the Los Angeles Memorial Coliseum, the damaged National Historic Landmark and international symbol of Los Angeles, the site of two Olympic Games. All of this was made possible by FEMA funds provided through the Office of Emergency Services to the Office of Historic Preservation.

Another response change was the increased use of computer technology. Within hours of the disaster, the Office of Historic Preservation's database of historic properties in the area was electronically transferred to the Office of Emergency Services/FEMA disaster center, and to local governments and key preservation organizations. The data were electronically compared against the tally of some 8,000 damaged properties in the City of Los Angeles.

This resulted in a list of 171 endangered historic buildings in Los Angeles alone: 58 red-tagged and 113 yellow-tagged. Preservationists could then focus their efforts on these identified endangered properties and be sure that the owners were provided with correct information, as well as needed assistance.

Shortly after the initial disaster, representatives of the Office of Historic Preservation and the State Historical Building Safety Board inspected historic buildings and posted their own determinations of the degree of damage. City inspectors usually concurred with these postings.

Local government contacts were quickly established and assistance provided by local preservation organizations, the state, or the National Trust for Historic Preservation, which has had a active role in the recent California disasters. Lists of historical architects and engineers experienced with earthquakes were also electronically distributed.

Local governments were quickly notified of their responsibilities under Public Resources Code 5028. We are now expecting only about ten requests for demolition from the City of Los Angeles alone.

A significant victory was the initial US$5 million provided by Congress for damaged historic properties, with the help of the California Governor's Office and the National Trust; this was an amazing accomplishment! US$1.5 million was set aside for planning and US$3.5 million for bricks and mortar (repair of damage) projects.

To administer the new grant program, a partnership was established, which included the Getty Conservation Institute, the California Preservation Foundation and the Los Angeles Conservancy, as well as the National Park Service, the National Trust and the Office of Historic Preservation. Normal federal granting requirements were modified to increase the applicability of the money. Grant applicants requested almost twice the amount of money available. Several months later, Congress provided a another US$5 million for local assistance.

Northridge was the first major earthquake to occur directly beneath a highly urbanized area in California. Due to public safety concerns, Governor Wilson ordered that the Seismic Safety Commission review the effects of the Northridge Earthquake and to study policy implications arising from the disaster, with particular attention to seismic structural safety and building design standards. The study specifically included historic structures.

The study found that historic buildings are not only valuable community cultural resources, but important parts of the local housing stock and economic infrastructure; and because older buildings are concentrated in traditional downtowns, their damage and loss will have disastrous long-term impacts on the speed of the recovery and economic viability.

Most importantly, the study concluded that the retrofitted unreinforced masonries generally performed well during the Northridge Earthquake, and that financial resources must be made available to seismically retrofit these buildings.

The lessons of the Loma Prieta Earthquake were well learned by California's preservationists. Although it helped that the Northridge Earthquake occurred in an area with a very strong preservation network, significant policy and procedural changes were made in the official response to the disaster.

Much more needs to be done, such as increasing disaster preparedness, providing seismic retrofit incentives and improving disaster mitigation and response. An adequate funding source for seismic retrofit does not yet exist, although there is currently legislation being considered, Senate Bill 875, which would provide tax credits for seismic retrofit. Unfortunately, there is no written disaster emergency plan in the State Office of Historic Preservation.

Furthermore, the Office has been unable to be actively involved with the Office of Emergency Services in disaster training and preparedness. Nevertheless, the Office of Historic Preservation and the preservation community in California have been able to clearly demonstrate their desire and ability to provide improved disaster assistance.

As David Look and many others have stated, we can be certain that disasters will continue to occur. The challenge for all of us is to determine what we can do now to protect our historic sites before, during and after a disaster, and how we can best develop proper response plans for future disasters.

Bibliography

Feilden, B. M. (1987) *Between two earthquakes. Cultural Property in Seismic Zones*, Getty Conservation Institute, Marine del Rey, California.

Donaldson, Milford Wayne (1998) 'The first ten days emergency response and protection strategies for the preservation of historic structures', in *Disaster Management Programs for Historic Sites*, eds Dirk H. R. Spennemann & David W. Look. San Francisco and Albury: Association for Preservation Technology (Western Chapter) and The Johnstone Centre, Charles Sturt University. Pp. 25-29.

4

The first ten days: emergency response and protection strategies for the preservation of historic structures

MILFORD WAYNE DONALDSON [¶]

The majority of all decisions for the disposition of earthquake-damaged historic structures are made within the first ten days of a declared national emergency. The devastating effects of the 17 January 1994 Northridge Earthquake on historic buildings showed once again that strategies for the preservation of these unique resources are at the mercy of local, state and federal agencies. Alternative preservation strategies are needed to complement the post-disaster public safety recovery and reconstruction methods already in place during the disaster period. The declared emergency may last from thirty to ninety days.

Following the declaration of emergency by the President of the United States upon request by the Governor of the State, there is a myriad of federal, state and local laws, codes, ordinances and policies that are implemented within two to three days that set the stage for decision-making. Although local agencies begin search and rescue methods to protect life, the greatest threat to historic structures are policies set by the Federal Emergency Management Agency (FEMA) and the State Office of Emergency Services.

The Applied Technology Council-20 red 'unsafe' placards, the suspension of protection under the California Environmental Quality Act, conservative attitudes of liability-conscious

[¶] Architect, Milford Wayne Donaldson and Associates,530 Sixth Street, Suite 100, San Diego, CA 92101, USA. E-mail: 73410.2250@compuserve

assessment volunteers unfamiliar with historical or older building construction, the rush to secure the 'limited' FEMA funds for demolition and the unfortunate interpretation of 'imminent threat' to bodily harm or damage to adjacent property continue to destroy historic buildings. In the case of historical structures, where damage following a moderate seismic event will always be present, the attitude is that a damaged building is dangerous and should be demolished. Many damaged historical buildings are torn down to be replaced with a 'replica'. Unfortunately, the concept of replication is becoming popular, even amongst the preservation community.

For federally funded projects, the Section 106 process does not become effective until after thirty days of the declaration of an emergency. The administration time required by the State Historic Preservation Officer (SHPO) is overwhelming and the staff cannot service the number of requests. In the case of the Northridge Earthquake, SHPO contracted with a private firm to oversee and review over 2,000 applications under Section 5028 of the State of California Public Resources Code. However, the determination of 'imminent threat' continues to be made at the local level and usually within five to seven days the decision to remove the threat has been finalized.

Throughout the last twelve years, there has been a great deal of effort and understanding for the preservation of historic buildings of the various local, state and federal agencies. However, the greatest protection comes from education and preparedness of the local decision makers. Since there are few historic structures noted on local, state or national registers within California, it may be possible to predetermine the disaster response methodology far in advance of the event. At the very least, the local city or county disaster ordinance should identify the procedures of dealing with historic buildings and be prepared with an updated list of the historic structures within the region.

The emergency response and protection strategies that should be implemented within the first ten days following a seismic event for the preservation of historic buildings are the following:

1. A knowledgeable team consisting of a preservationist, structural engineer and preservation architect familiar with older construction methods should be 'on-line' and aware of the locations of the historic resources on a regional basis. The structural engineer and architect should be registered as a Disaster Service Worker with the Office of Emergency Services. This team should be in addition to the County's Department of General Services Historic Resources Team.

2. Permission should be obtained to assess the damage to the historic structure from the local agency in charge of disaster recovery and the assessment team should be allowed to report directly to the owner the recommendations for restoration or stabilization and provide cost estimates.

3. Informational brochures should be available for local disaster personnel describing policies, laws and ordinances applicable to historical buildings. Recommended information should be at least the following:

   • National Historic Preservation Act, Section 106 process;

- Programmatic Agreements (if available) between FEMA, Office of Emergency Services, SHPO and the National Advisory Council for Historic Preservation;

- Joint FEMA/Office of Emergency Services Section 406 (Stafford Act) Hazard Mitigation Policy Statement;

- State Historical Building Code and the State Historical Building Safety Board's jurisdiction and appeal process;

- Section 5028 of the California Public Resources Code and related California Environmental Quality Act issues;

- California Seismic Safety Commission's *Retrofit Incentives for Local Government*;

- The Local Disaster Response Ordinance with emphasis on historic buildings;

- The Secretary of the Interior's Standards and Guidelines for the Rehabilitation of Historic Buildings.

4. All decisions regarding demolition, partial demolition or repair methods resulting in a significant loss of historic fabric to the historical resource should receive a qualified second opinion.

5. Promote the shoring and stabilization of 'imminent hazards' by initiating a working collaboration with the Urban Search and Rescue Team through the US Army Corps of Engineers and Office of Emergency Services. FEMA provides reimbursement of engineering fees and material costs for temporary measures. Attempt to salvage *all* historic fabric and store in the resource, including loose or fallen pieces.

6. Promote the transfer of sale to an interested party if an owner does not want to restore his/her historic building. Unfortunately, the State Building Seismic Program recommends replacement of a historical building when the retrofitted cost exceeds the Benefit Cost Ratio of 120% of the new cost. Although this percentage is much better than the 60% normal building profile, many of the retrofit cost estimates are not made by knowledgeable persons with extensive experience in retrofitting historic buildings. For state-owned historic buildings, the Division of the State Architect and the SHPO must be involved in the review process.

7. A separate and distinct damage assessment placard for historic resources should be provided. Recommendations should always include permanent protection from inclement weather and potential aftershocks. With publicly-owned historic buildings, the process to initiate repair may take as long as twelve to sixteen months.

8. During the discussion of the retrofit methodology, the engineer should note that the objective of the program is to reduce hazard to life. Damage during a moderate seismic event should be expected at definite locations within most historic and older structures.

9. Establish a detailed response repair ordinance for the historic buildings within the region, including permanent seismic strengthening methods to mitigate 'imminent threats' to life safety and damage to adjacent properties.

10. Provide guidance for the sensitive mitigation of hazardous materials during the disaster assessment. The removal of asbestos-containing materials, lead-based paints, pigeon dung, bat guano and other health hazards have resulted in the removal of the historic fabric during the 'clean-up' phase.

In summary, during the 'crisis management' phase following a seismic event, the preservation of historic resources becomes the lowest priority of disaster-related activities for local, state and federal agencies. The programmatic responses and mandated processes are intact and generally not subject to change. The best way to implement preservation programs is to become part of the process and quickly provide educational information and qualified assessment personnel within the first ten days following the disaster.

Bibliography

Advisory Council on Historic Preservation (1986) *36 CFR Part 800: Protection of Historic Properties.*

California Preservation Foundation (1990) *Living on the Fault Line*, Workshops, Feb.-Mar.

California Preservation Foundation (1993) *The Writ is Mightier than the Wrecking Ball*, Workshop, Mar.

California Preservation Foundation (1990) Newsletter, Jan.

California Preservation Foundation (1994) Newsletter, Feb.

Department of General Services (1994) *State Building Seismic Program Recommendations*, Division of the State Architect, State of California, April.

Federal/State/Local Coordinating Office (1994) *Joint FEMA/OES Section 406 (Stafford Act) Hazard Mitigation Policy Statement*, Pasadena, CA., 16 Sept.

FEMA, OES, SHPO, NACHP (1994) *Northridge Programmatic Agreements*, 7 Feb.

Governor's Office of Planning and Research (1994) *CEQA and Historical Resources.* State of California, April.

Harthorn, Roy (1994) *The Post-Earthquake Safety Evaluation and Damage Repair Assessment of Historic Buildings*, Graduate Project, California State University, Northridge, CA., Dec.

Merritt, John (1990) *History at Risk. Loma Prieta: Seismic Safety and Historic Buildings*, California Preservation Foundation.

Office of Historic Preservation (1989-92) Public Resources Code Section 5020-5028 *et seq.*

State Historical Building Safety Board (1990) State Historical Building Code. H & SC Section 18950 *et seq.* Title 24, CCR, Part 8.

Kimmelman, Alex (1998) 'Cultural heritage and disaster management in Tucson, Arizona', in *Disaster Management Programs for Historic Sites*, eds Dirk H. R. Spennemann & David W. Look. San Francisco and Albury: Association for Preservation Technology (Western Chapter) and The Johnstone Centre, Charles Sturt University. Pp. 31-37.

5

Cultural heritage and disaster management in Tucson, Arizona

ALEX KIMMELMAN [¶]

There is a great diversity of cultural resources in America, in general, to say nothing of the sites which are important to local communities. One of the most important sites in Tucson, Arizona is 'El Tiradito', the Wishing Shrine. A fabled site in the Barrio Libre National Register Historic District, the shrine commemorates the demise of a man who died while in the commission of a mortal sin and was buried in unconsecrated soil. Legend has it that if one lights a candle at the shrine and makes a wish, the wish will come true if the candle is still burning in the morning. Over the years, El Tiradito has witnessed small seas of candles extending out into the street during some of the various crises of this century. In the 1970s, the listing of El Tiradito on the Register was a key factor in stopping a freeway plan that would have displaced both the shrine and three adjacent historic districts.

Another site of limited architectural value, but enormous historic significance, is today referred to as 'Slab City'. In 1942, Japanese citizens were relocated to an isolated site on the Gila Indian Reservation. Hundreds of Quonset huts and other structures were built to accommodate the internees. The buildings have long since disappeared; today only the concrete slabs and pillars testify to the existence of the camp. Much of the camp site has been destroyed or converted over to agricultural use. The Gila River Pima Indians are today taking necessary measures to protect and administer the remaining resources.

[¶] 1131 East Spring Street, Tucson, Arizona 85719, USA. E-mail: ajfmaz@azstarnet.com

Figure 5.1. Located on the west side of the South Main Avenue at the edge of Barrio Viejo and Barrio El Hoyo, El Teradito ('The Wishing Shrine') is one of the most important religious sites in Tucson, Arizona. It was placed on the National Register of Historic Places in 1976. (Photo: Alex Kimmelman 1997).

Locations of multiple copies and accessibility of surveys and inventories at the local level

During the last century, historic preservation efforts have resulted in the production of vast quantities of documentation on buildings, structures and sites. The 1992 Amendment to the National Historic Preservation Act further expanded the range of documentation by requiring eligibility determinations on non-registered properties. In just nine months in Tucson, preparation of the reports used in the Section 106 process have resulted in the survey and inventory of over 1,200 properties in nine working class barrios. The Section 106 documentation includes both detailed architectural assessment and a historic significance report.

Whichever type of documentation is created, the information is valuable to both the residents of historic areas and the community at large. To ensure maximum access to these records (which generally reside only in government repositories), local institutions should be provided with copies whenever possible. In the aftermath of a disaster, local availability of historic records can be expected to speed the process of stabilization and restoration. Even without a disaster, historic records can be a boon to educational institutions. Accordingly, programs should be established to provide a link between preservation organizations and local schools. Churches, neighborhood centers, health clinics and other local institutions may benefit from sharing historic information and also provide a point of public accessibility.

Figure 5.2. Butte Camp, Japanese Relocation Facility, Sacaton, Arizona, ca. 1943. (Photo courtesy Casa Grande Historical Society, Pima Gila River Indian Reservation).

Disaster assessment (both potential and post-disaster)

The most important aspect of planning is planning - the act of identifying potentialities and establishing procedures to the meet the need. While both the act and the product of planning are imperative, especially in recovering from a natural disaster, the need for adaptability and innovation in the field is no less vital. Some equate planning for disasters as somewhat akin to planning for war. In the latter, technology usually renders the experience of the previous war as unsuitable for fighting the current; in disasters, mother nature's chaos dictates the need for flexibility.

Differences in institutional culture cannot be understated when examining the various roles government agencies play in disaster recovery and cultural preservation. Institutional attitudes that consider natural disasters as nature's way of clearing away the accumulated refuse or 'unfit' constructs of man fall in well with the proponents of urban or community renewal without regard for the preservation of cultural resources.

The first requirement for local disaster planning is to identify the most likely types of disaster which might occur. In Tucson, Arizona, we are blessed with an environment which historically has not witnessed major disasters on the scale of the California earthquakes or Mississippi Valley floods. Damage in Tucson is most likely to be caused by wind or fire, and with regard to historic structures, the damage usually involves catastrophic loss of roofs. Because of the recognition of the principal damage, the City preservation office has taken steps to assist property owners after a disaster. Development Standards for the historic districts identify appropriate replacement materials to be used in restoration. Cooperation with local trade groups and organizations, such as Construction Specifications Institute, facilitates rapid access to product data and suppliers. Interaction with the local 'Who's Who in Contracting' directory allows for rapid access to a broad range of construction trades. Preservation, particularly when adobe is involved, often requires specialists; and separate lists of these individuals and companies have also been compiled. Sources of financial aid - grants, low-interest loans, tax credits - should likewise be compiled and made available to the public.

Figure 5.3. 'Slab City', Japanese Relocation Facility, Sacaton, Arizona. Concrete pillars mark the location of the Butte Camp and the buildings constructed here. (Photo: Alex Kimmelman 1995).

In the post-disaster environment, it is vital to document the condition of historic and cultural resources as soon as possible. This documentation should continue through various stages of the restoration. Procedures should be established to provide immediate approval for permits necessary to stabilize and protect property after a disaster. Fencing, shoring up, partial demolition to remove elements which may imperil public safety or adjacent properties should not be subject to extended review processes. Review boards need to be convened at the earliest time to provide assistance and/or clear restoration plans for permitting when appropriate. Property owners should be permitted to restore a structure to an identical condition as that which existed before the disaster. In this regard, local preservation agencies should develop programs to assist property owners make historic upgrades when they are not economically able to do so otherwise. In all cases, property owners' rights to existing conditions must be respected.

Figure 5.4. Rollings Sonoran Rowhouse, South Convent Avenue in El Libre National Register Historic District, Tucson, Arizona. Appearance of the building prior to wind damage and restoration. (Photo: Kelley Rollings 1980).

Stabilization, protection and repair of damaged historic sites

Restoration of historic properties following a natural disaster can illicit a wide array of preservation and building code issues. Such was the case following severe wind conditions in January 1993 which damaged historic buildings in El Libre National Register Historic District in Tucson, Arizona. Barrio Libre is a working class district, and thus has changed over time in a manner consistent of neighborhoods with similar economic and social conditions. Roof systems especially have been subject to major alterations over the years. Originally, all building in the district (some dating from the mid-1860s) had flat roofs with parapet walls. Between 1910 and 1930, with large quantities of building materials available, most property owners transformed their Sonoran rowhouses with the addition of sloped roofs. Secretary of Interior Standard for Rehabilitation, Number 4, states that additions and alterations over time may become historic in their own right and, if so, should be preserved. Consequently, local buildings may have traditionally had a flat/parapet configuration. But what if the - more recent - hipped roof is destroyed in a storm?

Such was the case for a property owned by Kelley Rollings, a long-time property owner and early preservationist in the Barrio. With the hipped roof lifted off the building and deposited in the middle of the street, the property owner was left with the reasonable option of restoring the roof to either historic configuration. Of course, before the new roof was installed, the building was brought up to code with the addition of a bond beam to tie the entire structure together. This type of situation is not unusual. More roofs are lost to fire than wind, but the situation remains essentially the same: namely, release permits to protect the remaining resources and facilitate an emergency review to deal with any changes sought in the restoration.

Figure 5.5. Rollings Sonoran Rowhouse, South Convent Avenue in El Libre National Register Historic District, Tucson, Arizona. Appearance of the fully restored building following the 1993 wind damage. (Photo: Alex Kimmelman 1997).

The Historic Preservation Office and building safety officials need to continually update the photographic documentation of each listed property. Experience in Tucson suggests that when roofs are being installed, inappropriate and non-historic elements such as skylights, modern venting systems and mechanical equipment mysteriously appear where none had existed before. Notation on plans regarding these elements are the first line of defense in promoting a true restoration of the historic building. However, only regular site inspections during construction will insure against intrusive elements being added in a conspicuous locations on a historic building.

A beneficial aspect may exist for education if preservation coordinators and property owners work quickly. While wall and roof systems lie exposed, it may be possible to provide training programs to those involved in local preservation activities: historic review boards, construction programs in public schools and community colleges and university architectural departments.

Alfaro, Jorge (1998) 'The role of federal disaster relief
assistance to local communities for historic preservation',
in *Disaster Management Programs for Historic Sites,* eds
Dirk H. R. Spennemann & David W. Look. San
Francisco and Albury: Association for Preservation
Technology (Western Chapter) and The Johnstone
Centre, Charles Sturt University. Pp. 39-42.

6

The role of federal disaster relief assistance to local communities for historic preservation

JORGE ALFARO ¶

Immediately after the 17 October 1989 Loma Prieta Earthquake, the City and County of San Francisco began the preparation of a local bond proposal which would give San Franciscans the opportunity to recover from the earthquake damage to city-owned buildings much quicker than other surrounding communities. In June 1990, the voters of San Francisco passed a US$332.4 million General Obligation Bond Issue to fund the repair of city-owned buildings and seismically upgrade some of them in preparation for the next major earthquake.

The effort of putting together and passing bond proposals for the seismic upgrade of city buildings was nothing new to San Francisco. In 1987 and 1989, two separate bond proposals had already funded the seismic upgrade of police stations, fire stations, museums and hospital infrastructure facilities. Later on, in 1992 and 1994, two other bond proposals were approved for the seismic upgrade of more fire stations and one museum. All these funding commitments by the voters made San Francisco a leader in preserving the heritage of public infrastructure built in the early part of the century. Thus, when the Federal Emergency Management Agency (FEMA) and California's Office of Emergency Services entered the picture after the Loma Prieta Earthquake, the City was ready to move on with the repair and upgrade projects.

¶ Chief of Staff, Department of Public Works, San Francisco, California, CA 94102, USA

Figure 6.1. The historic school building at Merizio, Guam, severely damaged during Typhoon Ross in September 1992. The lack of funding to restore the structure saw the continued decay of a historically significant building. (Photo: Dirk Spennemann 1994).

The City's relationship with FEMA and the Office of Emergency Services during the recovery period was collaborative as well as typically bureaucratic. A massive paper trail was needed to keep hundreds of projects on target with a high rate of success unforeseen in prior disaster recovery efforts. Two good examples of the collaborative effort between FEMA & Office of Emergency Services and San Francisco for the preservation of historic structures were the US$3.1 million seismic upgrade of the 1895 Spreckels Temple of Music in Golden Gate Park and the US$24 million seismic upgrade and expansion of the 1924 Palace of the Legion of Honor in Lincoln Park.

The Bureau of Architecture of the Department of Public Works designed and managed the Spreckels Temple of Music project. Page and Trumbull did initial preservation feasibility studies while Carcy and Company provided consultation to the Bureau of Architecture during design and construction. The project required the complete realignment of colonnades while reinforcing the main central structure. What was unique about this project, besides being the recipient of multiple awards, was that FEMA & Office of Emergency Services reimbursed the City for almost 100% of the project costs and the building was restored in time for its centennial celebration.

Barnes and Cavagnero designed and oversaw construction of the Palace of the Legion of Honor project. As opposed to the Spreckels project, given the fact that the Loma Prieta damage was limited to cracks in concrete beams, scaggliola-finished stairways and the displacement of sixteen marble non-structural columns, FEMA & Office of Emergency

Services only funded approximately 1% of the cost of construction. Nevertheless, there was high level of scrutiny by State Historic Preservation Office (SHPO), FEMA and the Office of Emergency Services of the entire upgrade and expansion 'undertaking' even though Federal disaster assistance was very minimal. In the end, the building was restored and expanded within SHPO's guidelines and its re-opening was a big success from every viewpoint.

In summary, regardless of FEMA & Office of Emergency Services funding commitments following a natural disaster, local communities have an obligation to take the lead in procuring for themselves the resources needed to preserve the cultural heritage and protect historically significant public buildings. In addition, historic buildings should be preserved not to become museum pieces in the urban landscape, but to be enriched by human activity and purpose. In San Francisco's case, every building which is preserved is being used to its fullest and will continue to do so for the next century. Together with the community, the Bureau of Architecture makes every effort to preserve San Francisco's character and its historic civic architecture for the 21st century.

Figure 6.2. The historic school building at Merizio, Guam, severely damaged during Typhoon Ross in September 1992. Note the decay at left brought about by the loss of the roof and subsequent exposure to tropical sun and rain. (Photo: Dirk Spennemann 1994).

Figure 6.3. Mission Kampanayun Malessu at Merizio, Guam, severely damaged by an earthquake which occurred during Typhoon Ross in September 1992. The lack of funding to restore the structure and the wind-damaged roof saw the continued decay of a historically significant building. (Photo: Dirk Spennemann 1994).

THE RECOGNITION OF SIGNIFICANT HISTORIC CHARACTER AND FABRIC IN A POST-DISASTER SITUATION

Siekkinen, George O. Jr. (1998) 'The recognition of
significant historic character and fabric', in *Disaster
Management Programs for Historic Sites*, eds Dirk H. R.
Spennemann & David W. Look. San Francisco and
Albury: Association for Preservation Technology
(Western Chapter) and The Johnstone Centre, Charles
Sturt University. Pp. 45-48.

7

The recognition of significant historic character and fabric

GEORGE O. SIEKKINEN JR. [¶]

When I first received the request to participate in this disaster symposium, I grappled with
how to get a handle on the title in a meaningful fashion. I tried to determine what approach
to take, how to discuss it and how to put into context so we can understand it. The concept
of historic character and its relationship to the historic fabric of buildings and structures is
probably a concept that we often do not think about, but there are other things that we think
about and some comparison may prove beneficial to our understanding of the meaning of
historic character and fabric for historic buildings.

How many of us are collectors? How many collect something? Just think about that in
terms of the genre of whatever you collect. Do you collect antique cars, guns, stamps,
books, works of art on paper, bronzes, oil paintings, antique furniture, or painted
furniture? You get the nuances and ideas of that genre of collection and you very quickly
become aware of the fact that original character, original fabric, original material adds
greatly to the intrinsic value of the object you collect, which you love and which you spend
time trying to find. The idea that you would change that character, alter that fabric, or
modify that original material for a personal or aesthetic reason is something you would
recognize today as being a great mistake. This is because most collectors know that such
alterations or modifications to original character and fabric will most likely degrade the
intrinsic value of the object and will probably lower the economic value of the object.

[¶] Historical Architect, National Trust for Historic Preservation, 1785 Massachusetts Avenue, NW, Washington,
DC 20036, USA
Note: The text for this contribution was composed by the sessional organizer George Siekkinen, drawing on a
videotape of the actual talk presented at the session. His contribution is expressly acknowledged.

Figure 7.1. St. John's Church, Inarajan, Guam, severely damaged in September 1992 by the dual effects of Typhoon Ross and an earthquake which occurred at the same time. This church is one of the few buildings surviving from the pre-World War II period of Guam and has a very high cultural and historic significance. Note toppled spire ornament and missing roof sections. (Photo: Dirk Spennemann 1994).

Let us say that you had a piece of painted furniture and you had stripped it of its original paint finish (from the 18th or early 19th century). On taking that piece to the market to sell, you would probably encounter someone who would say to you that you stripped the original paint off that 'Pennsylvania German cupboard' and stained it a dark walnut color, but underneath there is a remnant of the original blue paint. You would be accused of seriously degrading the piece and lowering the price you could have received for it.

Why we treat historic buildings differently is the next philosophical question. Continuing this line of logic, we have an object, we have collections, and we value those things 'as is'. We protect those things as is, so why do we treat historic buildings any differently? Why do we say, "Let's rip out the storefront; let's cover the cast iron columns of the storefront with some modern material. Let's take out the Luxfer prism transom lights and replace them with something different".

Why do we deal with historic buildings in such a different fashion? How do we make the connection for historic buildings with the idea that in protecting an antique we understand that protecting its intrinsic value will also protect its economic value to us? Part of the reason for treating buildings so differently, is that we view buildings as functional objects: we live in them, we work in them, we use them.

Figure 7.2. St. John's Church, Inarajan, Guam. Minor damage to reinforced concrete column. This damage is repairable and should not result in the loss of a historically significant structure. (Photo: Dirk Spennemann 1994).

So in a sense, on a depreciation schedule, we theoretically use the buildings up and then discard them. We need to expand our sense of how we approach historic buildings and how we look at their historic fabric, materials and systems.

These are the philosophical questions I wish to pose. My own progress in this has been greatly encouraged from my interactions with my colleagues at the National Trust, such as the curator and the archaeologist.

Figure 7.3. St. John's Church, Inarajan, Guam. The earthquake revealed an earlier attempt at seismic retrofitting the buttresses through reinforcement. (Photo: Dirk Spennemann 1994).

8
Assessing the character and systems of historic buildings

E. BLAINE CLIVER [¶]

Obviously when a disaster has occurred, it will be too late to conduct the assessment of the historic character and fabric of a building. The following case study is about an event that occurred about thirteen years ago while I was in a previous job in Boston.

I received a phone call at four o'clock in the morning from one of my employees who was working at the Roosevelt Historic Site in Hyde Park, New York, and also supervising a project crew at Fire Island, New York . He had begun his Park Service career at that park and had worked there for about fifteen years before I hired him for the Charlestown Navy Yard. He called me, on the verge of tears, to say that President Franklin Delano Roosevelt's home at Hyde Park was on fire. This was something that was very difficult for him as he had put a great deal of his life into maintaining and preserving this site. I asked about the crew in Fire Island and he said that he would contact them and get them to come up to Hyde Park. I said that I would drive over as quickly as possible from Boston.

By the time I got there, the fire was out, much of the contents had been dealt with and were out of the house, and the crew was starting to put a temporary roof on the house. What the park had done in the past was very important in terms of minimizing the damage resulting from the fire. Specifically, the park had planned and exercised foresight in disaster planning and preparedness. Many of the volunteer firemen from the Hyde Park fire department were also employees of the Park Service. During the previous years, the park had many meetings with the fire department. There had also been tours for the volunteer

[¶] Chief, Preservation Assistance Division, National Park Service, PO Box 37127, Washington, DC 20013-7127, USA

Note: The text for this contribution was composed by the sessional organizer George Siekkinen, drawing on a videotape of the actual talk presented at the session. His contribution is expressly acknowledged.

firemen of the Franklin Delano Roosevelt Site and the nearby the Vanderbilt Historic Site. The fire department had been taken through the building and there had been many useful exchanges of information between the park staff and the fire department. The fire department volunteers and the park staff knew each other and the fire department volunteers knew what was important about the buildings and their contents. In addition, the park staff had set aside tarpaulins for use in the event of an emergency.

Thus, when the fire occurred, the park staff and the volunteer fire department were able to work well together. This was one of the few times where I have observed a fire department allowing non-fire department staff to go into a house during a fire. The park curators were allowed to go into the house and remove the paintings, artwork and other moveable items and put tarpaulins over the bigger pieces that could not be moved. All this happened while the fire department was still fighting the fire on the roof. The fire was extinguished without causing much additional damage to what the fire had caused. The fire department minimized the amount of water that was used and also minimized the number of holes that were cut into the roof. The Fire Island crew was able to begin working on the roof repairs and a temporary roof was installed by the end of that same day; the rains came, but the inside stayed dry without taking on any more water. The park staff began drying things out and started cleaning the inside. In the long run, the house survived with minimal damage.

What was interesting was the process of estimating what it would cost to undertake the repairs. I managed to have the Fire Island crew leader and the chief of maintenance of the park, who usually fought like 'cats and dogs', to sit down with me to develop the estimate, which ended up being about US$1 million. We contracted out the structural work on the roof as quickly as possible; the park service crews did the cleaning of the finishes and painting on the first and second floors; the roof was done by a contractor; and, in the end, it all came together quite easily. One important element that was on hand before any of the repair work commenced were the Historic American Building Survey drawings which had been completed many years before. These were available to the architectural firm we hired to develop the drawing for the roof work.

The fire at the Franklin Delano Roosevelt Mansion is a good example of a disaster where the planning and disaster preparedness work accomplished beforehand really paid off.

Donaldson, Milford Wayne (1998) 'Conserving the historic fabric: a volunteer disaster worker's perspective', in *Disaster Management Programs for Historic Sites*, eds Dirk H. R. Spennemann & David W. Look. San Francisco and Albury: Association for Preservation Technology (Western Chapter) and The Johnstone Centre, Charles Sturt University. Pp. 51-54.

9

Conserving the historic fabric: a volunteer disaster worker's perspective

MILFORD WAYNE DONALDSON [¶]

This discussion is from the perspective of a volunteer disaster worker as he or she goes out into the field after an earthquake and tries to determine if a particular building is dangerous or not.

It is unfortunate with our specialized training today that we have fragmented our common sense. We only react to building codes and laws and fail to keep common sense in mind. We only react to threats of liability. When San Diego was settled and started to grow in the late 19th century, many of the buildings surviving from that period are interesting examples of very different types of construction from different parts of the country. For instance, the San Diego Hardware Company building was exactly the same type of building as was built in Chicago. The owner of the hardware company brought his builder out from Chicago and had the Chicago building replicated. In importing these building practices, many of the immigrant builders did not take into account the potential for seismic activity in the West, and in California particularly.

In the example of the 1906 San Francisco Earthquake and Fire, the potential for seismic activity was known by the builders and many innovative techniques were used. We also have to acknowledge the skills of the people who built the early abodes around the state. In considering the example of the San Francisco City Hall, period photographs taken after the 1906 Earthquake and Fire show that most of the building's structural system was

[¶] Architect, Milford Wayne Donaldson and Associates, 530 Sixth Street, Suite 100, San Diego, CA 92101, USA. E-mail: 73410.2250@compuserve
Note: The text for this contribution was composed by the sessional organizer George Siekkinen, drawing on a videotape of the actual talk presented at the session. His contribution is expressly acknowledged.

constructed of cast iron and that it remained standing. Though the City Hall had lost major portions of its exterior masonry cladding, the building could probably have been repaired and rebuilt. However, the earthquake provided an excuse for the city's leaders to build a new city hall on a new site. Today we are dealing with how to seismic retrofit the current city hall. We have spent six years just coming to terms with how much it will cost to seismically retrofit the building and we will probably spend another six years to complete the project.

After any major earthquake, we have the major public issue of how to properly deal with the refugees and people who have lost access to their homes. In period photographs taken in San Francisco after the 1906 Earthquake and Fire, I wonder if some of the photographs were staged, because it seems to me that the refugees all appear to be rather well dressed, or perhaps people had a better sense of personal style and fashion in San Francisco in those days!

The Orange County Courthouse, in Santa Ana, California, is a spectacular example of how a County Supervisor can have his way. In this case, one of the County Supervisors had just moved to California from Arizona. He used his influence to have the building constructed from Arizona sandstone when most other projects were using native California stones at the time. One of the prominent features of the building was its central tower which appears to be made of sandstone. In the 1933 Earthquake, part of the gable wall over the front entrance fell down onto the front steps. It is interesting to notice that the 'sandstone' tower had survived the earthquake in fine condition and was still standing. I use this to make the point that the engineers of this time were not stupid. The American Society of Civil Engineers had been formed in 1852 and had been working to increase knowledge and standards of practice. The tower was actually made of pressed metal on a stamped sheet metal framework. It looked like it was constructed of sandstone, but it was really a very lightweight element in relative terms and would not pose such a great seismic risk as long as it was well connected to the building's structural system. Unfortunately, within seven days of the 1933 Earthquake, the Orange County Board of Supervisors had ordered the tower to be taken down when it probably did not have to be removed. Another important feature lost was the decorative gable. It was not replaced or restored and it is an example of the loss of character-defining features which we will probably never get back. The loss of such ornamentation is unfortunate especially as these items could not be included in the building's retrofit budget which exceeded US$32 million.

In downtown commercial buildings in Santa Ana, one observes interesting changes in the character, style and materials used on buildings as a result of past earthquakes. One sees many substitute materials in elements such as cornices. Many of these cornices are actually made of lightweight materials even though they were made to look like stone. In the case of the Santa Ana Earthquake in 1933, many commercial buildings from the late 19th and early 20th centuries had lost pieces of ornamentation. These lost elements were often not restored; rather, they were replaced with Art Deco-style features which were more fashionable at the time. This trend was so striking that today the period of significance for the downtown historic district now includes evidence of the 1933 Earthquake and the remodeling work that was done after it. One finds in the district many earthquake period Art Deco storefronts attached to buildings with more classical or earlier architectural styles visible on the upper floors.

In the case of the 1925 Earthquake in Santa Barbara, a group of leading citizens decided to change the entire architectural style and character of the town. They decided to rebuild the town in the Spanish revival style. They called on experts such as a Messrs. Winslow and Weeper. Some of the experts had been representatives who had traveled and promoted the use of Portland cement. The extensive use of the Mission and Spanish revival styles that we now have in Santa Barbara was a trend that could have happened up and down the coast.

The impact of earthquakes is given a great deal of coverage in the media with graphic images portrayed of buildings which have collapsed. The media coverage tends to exacerbate the real dimensions of the event. There have been very serious disasters in many countries, but I really believe that in California there are good engineers, good building codes and good buildings when you compare the number of people killed in earthquakes in California to other countries.

After the Mexico City Earthquake, John Kariotis and I went down to see the aftermath. We saw multi-story buildings that had keeled over. There was one 22-story building which had been built after World War II when structural steel was not available, so box beams were welded up to take the place of the structural steel. Unfortunately, the building was not strong enough to withstand the earthquake, and it collapsed.

However, one saw examples of Spanish Colonial period building with clock towers and constructed of unreinforced masonry which had survived and were standing next to the ruins of a 1950s building which had totally collapsed.

We need to consider the types of earthquakes that happen in California. The important thing to keep in mind is that so many decisions are made within ten days after an earthquake. So many buildings are lost in the short period immediately after an earthquake because of the short time frame and the rush to make decisions. Too many buildings are needlessly demolished in this rushed period of action after an earthquake.

Today we have fragmented our education and training. We need to need to rethink how we have organized our training and education systems. We need to revive the various buildings manuals from the 19th and early 20th centuries to find illustrations of how historic buildings were built in what was considered the best practice of the day.

In historic buildings, we have many structures which are mixtures of different buildings materials such as brick, concrete, metal and wood. We find construction details such as soldier courses and other details in brick work and poured-in-place concrete lintels over windows and doors. We can find buildings with a brick exterior on the facade and terracotta block on the interior and these are completely hiding the structural steel framework of the building. This type of building could be mislabeled an unreinforced masonry building. The practice of the day was for hollow terracotta blocks not to be used as a primary structural system except for one-story buildings. In multi-story buildings, terracotta blocks were used for fireproofing the steel structural system, but too many were torn down needlessly.

After an earthquake, emergency period laws such as the declaration of an 'imminent threat' based on the Public Resources Code Section 5028 are implemented. I have seen examples of this ordinance being used to declare an imminent threat where a brick parapet had already fallen into the street. The building suffered nothing else - not even one broken window. This was the only grocery store in the town and the building was quickly demolished causing great hardship for the community. This was based on the idea that the building presented some sort of imminent threat when, in fact, whatever threat that had existed had been lost in the first moments of the earthquake when the brick parapet fell over.

In other examples of what could happen to historic buildings in the event of an earthquake, one see windows frames that are not well connected. In a house in Ferndale, California, the house has fallen over on its cripple wall in several previous earthquakes and each time it has been put back up on a new cripple wall. In some instances, damage to houses is ascribed to the earthquake when the real cause is the lack of proper maintenance. The risk of the collapse of the first story onto the cripple story of the basement is often observed. Many people think that wooden frame buildings are safer in the event of an earthquake, but this is not necessarily true unless the building's structural system is well tied together. Another thing to keep in mind is that many connections in a building's structural system may be hidden from view such as blind fastening on structural trusses.

In many buildings, there are particular points of weakness. In one apartment building, the building had been partially retrofitted. One corner of the building provided the location for the plumbing chase for the kitchens and bathrooms, so that at the bottom there was only one wythe of brick. In the earthquake, this weak point was what gave way and throughout most of the rest of the building there was very little damage. The building was torn down when it could have been repaired.

We are just starting to acknowledge that brick veneers can be very dangerous if they become detached from the supporting plates during the vibrations of the building during an earthquake. Brick veneers need to be carefully anchored into the building's structural system. We recognize that hollow terracotta clay blocks have always been a problem, but many of the block walls have concrete bond beams and anchor bolts which are not visible from the exterior.

With the old Masonic Lodge Building in Fillmore, California, one saw similar problems with collapse in plumbing chase locations. These could have been easily repaired, but what had been the greatest building in Fillmore was lost within seven days after an earthquake through needless demolition.

At the San Diego Mission, there is a structure which is mostly reinforced concrete which was built during the 1930s as a Civilian Conservation Corps public works project. Only one room at the Mission was constructed of adobe, yet it was erroneously labeled as an unreinforced masonry building by the city planning department.

In addition to the issues associated with earthquakes and how we react to them and damaged historic buildings, we also have problems with our reactions to floods. At the Santa Margarita rancho, which was taken over by the Marine Corps for use as Camp Pendleton in 1942, a recent flood damaged one of the original adobe buildings. Luckily, the base commander's wife was an ardent preservationist and the building was restored using the traditional materials and techniques.

As a final word, keep in mind that a disaster is like a disease: the longer it stays, the more difficult it becomes. It becomes like a blind date that won't go away.

Kariotis, John (1998) 'The tendency to demolish repairable structures in the name of 'life safety'', in *Disaster Management Programs for Historic Sites*, eds Dirk H. R. Spennemann & David W. Look. San Francisco and Albury: Association for Preservation Technology (Western Chapter) and The Johnstone Centre, Charles Sturt University. Pp. 55-60.

10

The tendency to demolish repairable structures in the name of 'life safety'

This discussion examines the behavior of buildings that have unreinforced masonry. This class of buildings is some of the most vulnerable in that the masonry is unique. It is brittle, low in tensile value and is often deemed to constitute a hazard when it is severely damaged. In my opinion, the damaged historic buildings do not often constitute a hazard after the earthquake event has already passed. I do not see how these can be found to present a risk and I cannot see a reason for the demolition of damaged historic buildings as a result of an earthquake. I believe that the demolition of historic buildings is often a decision made for reasons unrelated to life safety.

We have repaired many buildings damaged during the 1994 Northridge Earthquake. One modern building remained fully occupied even though twenty out of eighty of its structural columns had been broken during the earthquake. We repaired it and kept it occupied because we did not believe that it constituted a significant life safety hazard.

If we can do that to ordinary office buildings then we can certainly do the same to historic buildings. The decision to repair a historic buildings should take into account all the factors known. In my opinion, the decision to demolition a building based on life safety threats is often based on reasons that are not related to true life safety threats.

When we talk about the life safety threats posed by earthquakes, we are really talking about a threat that is so small compared to all other threats to life safety that the earthquake life safety threat is totally insignificant. In the Northridge Earthquake, the total count of lives

---

[¶] Structural Engineer, Kariotis & Associates, 711 Mission Street, Suite D, South Pasadena, CA 91030, USA

Note: The text for this contribution was composed by the sessional organizer George Siekkinen, drawing on a videotape of the actual talk presented at the session. His contribution is expressly acknowledged.

lost related to building failure was twenty-eight. At the same time, 45,000 people a year are killed on our roads and we do nothing about it. Why then are we so concerned with life safety threats from earthquakes? The answer is the preservation of historic buildings.

Consider a historic building not designed for an earthquake. This building comprises a concrete frame with masonry infill cladding. It has a response in a probable earthquake that is not related to any code building. I have heard arguments about the San Francisco City Hall and whether it should it be reconstructed to today's code. The answer for it and this concrete-frame building is that these buildings were built to some prior building code.

The important difference is that building codes are primarily for the construction of a new building. It has nothing to do with the analysis and determination of life safety risks posed by an existing building. Existing buildings are analyzed to see if they constitute a significant risk for damage during an earthquake. Now an earthquake is an unusual thing; we determine the intensity of earthquake shaking on a probabilistic basis and define what is considered for new buildings as an acceptable risk. In other words, we think that some failure is to be anticipated. We think this because we do not get to control the horizontal structural loading that occurs during an earthquake. The loading is random and varies greatly with sites only a few blocks apart as observed in the overview of damage in the Loma Prieta, Northridge and San Fernando Earthquakes. This is because ground motion energy is arriving in real time at a site and this energy can combine with energy arriving from another point on the fault system or it can cancel each other out. As we record ground motions at sites a few blocks apart, the results are significantly different. Since we cannot control the loading, we do have to define the risks in a probabilistic manner. We have procedures for reducing life safety threats. How do we reduce life safety threats? We reduce them by reducing damage. The response to an earthquake of a hotel in downtown Los Angeles consisting of a steel frame building with several wings is related to its steel frame and the unreinforced masonry infill; and its response is not covered in any code whatsoever. This building has essentially little or no damage observed as a result of the recent earthquake activity in Los Angeles.

In a sense, a historic building is really the entire building including all its material. The following discussion will show how to relate the historic fabric in a building to its historic character.

Take the example of the famous flat-iron shaped building on Columbus Avenue in San Francisco. Its style and its character are totally related to its historic fabric. Another example would be the Quincy Markets in Boston, Massachusetts. It has a facade which is composed of cut stone dry laid, but it has been altered as it has concrete floors on the interior. I do not know when these interior modifications were done. The exterior is original and it is cut Vermont granite. It is an example of one of those unreinforced masonry buildings. The question is whether it is stable and the answer is "Yes, it is". Those blocks of granite stacked on top of one another have a high potential for staying stable. The structure need not be renovated or replicated. What we have to recognize is that if we were to have an earthquake of the magnitude to damage it, it should be repaired. We repair buildings after fires, floods and all other disasters. I think that we ought to treat earthquake-damaged buildings in the same fashion and recognize that we will very likely have to repair them.

Figure 10.1. Site of the former Oddfellows Hall, Watsonville, CA. The building was damaged during the Loma Prieta Earthquake and was demolished even though it would have been repairable. Two years later the site remains vacant, a typical situation where local economies and lack of funding prevented a quick recovery and new construction to replace demolished retail buildings. (Photo: Steade Craigo 1991).

The Orange County Courthouse, as discussed by Donaldson (this volume), has been renovated to reduce its potential hazard. Its real problem was something that survived the other earthquake - namely, the very high second story. The second story walls are very tall and vary from seventeen to twenty feet in height and are only three wythes of brick thick. These walls had the potential for being unstable. The exterior facade has been preserved. Unfortunately, we could not get the restoration of the central tower which had been removed after the 1930s Earthquake. There were not sufficient funds available (as is often the case).

The idea of some potential for damage in historic buildings actually got me into trouble with the county engineer. There was a minor earthquake in Santa Ana and a newspaper reporter from the *Los Angeles Times* called to inquire if I was going to look at my building. The reporter said that there had been an earthquake in Santa Ana and that the City Hall was closed. I said that nothing would have happened to the courthouse and this remark was published. The county engineer misinterpreted my remark to infer that I was making a derogatory remark about the City Hall as compared to the County Courthouse.

A theater in Salt Lake City has a facade composed of terracotta blocks. The entire facade has recently been restored with various blocks recast. The historic character of this building is derived from its historic terracotta facade. The terracotta blocks are very brittle and the question is whether there can be anything done to protect these terracotta blocks from the potential damage resulting from an earthquake along the Wasatch Range.   Can I do anything to keep these blocks from getting cracks or some damage? The answer is "no", but this does not mean that the building has to be demolished. The damaged terracotta blocks can be easily repaired. The terracotta blocks could be cast again for the third time if need be.

Consider the example of a very ornate Romanesque revival masonry structure in the eastern United States. It has tall chimneys, towers and corner elements that, together with its basic shape, make it very complex. It is a very different type of structure from what would be designed and constructed today. In this building, one has to consider the tower masses and large mass elements on the corners. It has roofs with very steep pitches that do not really constitute a tie at the top. This presents a problem in that there is the potential for some damage occurring, but we have the techniques and abilities to repair such damage. However, we hear the argument that because one cannot prevent future damage from occurring in some future earthquake, we must demolish these historic buildings now.

The Union Station in Saint Louis has been adaptively re-used to serve as a shopping mall and hotel. The building has a very complex shape with its very tall tower and its various ornamental embellishments in masonry could constitute a severe problem if we want to minimize damage. We can minimize the potential for damage to the point where the damage is repairable and that is the concept on which we have to focus.

The Bradbury Building in downtown Los Angeles is another historic building that my firm has worked on in its renovation. This is a unique building in that it has a wood floor structural system and exterior masonry walls. Its floor plan is actually a donut with a large atrium in the center. The real problem of this building is its exterior sandstone which was quarried locally in California. The stone is not holding up compared with some other sandstones such as the Arizona sandstone used in the Orange County Courthouse. Ninety years later, we have some severe problems with the Bradbury Building and the deterioration of the sandstone facade.

The Pasadena City Hall presents an interesting case: computer modeling analysis of potential earthquake risks has been executed for this building. The building's analysis indicated that it could not survive the intensity of earthquake ground motions similar to what it already has undergone in various previous earthquakes. In the computer model used, it you do not enter the proper data on the materials used you will get silly answers. In this building, its large domed tower is considered a potential hazard. I cannot really understand this hazard analysis as the tower is constructed of reinforced concrete and in the middle of the tower legs there are massive structural steel members. I do not understand how one could have a shear failure through such a piece of structural steel. I see this as an example of where the computer analysis of potential earthquake risk can grossly overestimate the potential damage that the ground motions would cause when the building has already survived such ground motions without suffering any damage.

Right now, we are repairing one of the adobes in the San Fernando Valley that was damaged in the Northridge Earthquake. It was repaired previously in 1932 by a man named Harrington. He used tractional adobe techniques and also reinforced it with barbed wire. We are following the same approach except we are not using barbed wire because it will rust so we are using stainless steel wire. I see no reason that the adobe can not be repaired again if the San Fernando Valley were to be so unlucky as to have another earthquake within the next twenty or thirty years. The adobe had been the residence of Andreas Pico. Harrington used it as his residence and now it is a historic house museum. We are going to keep using these historic buildings. Many of the buildings I discussed have been extensively rehabilitated but that their historic character still remains. There historic buildings need to be used in order to preserve them.

By way of conclusion, I wish to reiterate that we need to prevent the needless demolition of historic buildings. I cannot see why we have any arguments about why we have to demolish historic buildings. Demolish is not the type of thing that has to be accomplished within a short time immediately after an earthquake - say, within six to nine days after an earthquake. We have to recognize that we are going to repair buildings.

We seem to have developed a strange view about what is hazardous. Further, I find it curious that we will not allow the general public to walk on the sidewalks in front of some damaged historic buildings after an earthquake, but we allow construction crews to go into these buildings. Are the construction laborers expendable and the general public is not? I was told that I could not walk down Main Street after the 1989 Loma Prieta Earthquake because of the risk that the front facades of the buildings could fall over and reach the centerline of the street. When I wished to examine these buildings, I was told by a policeman that it was too dangerous. A fire captain who was present said that, in his opinion, these buildings were *not* hazardous. He was used to going into a damaged building when it is on fire. These buildings were not on fire and had survived the earthquake and he did not see the potential for hazard.

We have developed a view that we must demolish historic buildings after an earthquake, but I believe that the reasons often have to do with something other than public safety. The issue of public safety is so small for buildings from earthquake hazards presented by buildings constructed in the United States (in particular, the western United States) compared with Mexico City, the Philippines, Russia or Armenia that I do not really think that earthquake risk in historic buildings really constitutes a hazard that threatens life compared to all the other hazards we face in daily life. We need get the message across to all people and all government agencies that we need to stop this idea that we need to demolish historic buildings immediately after an earthquake because of public safety risks. I recognize that not all historic buildings will necessarily be repaired after an earthquake. The decision on whether to repair or not should be made considering all the information and that the over use of the public safety issue should be minimized.

Bibliography

Donaldson, W. (1998) *The first ten days: emergency response and protection strategies for the preservation of historic structures*, this volume.

Figure 10.2. St. Patrick's Catholic Church, Watsonville, CA. The church was partially damaged during Loma Prieta in 1989. Because the congregation could not afford the necessary repairs and seismic retrofit the church was demolished and a new church constructed on the same site. The metal steeple was removed first because emergency officials feared the structure would topple in aftershocks, blocking a nearby main traffic route. (Photo: Steade Craigo 1989).

SEISMIC SAFETY AND REHABILITATION

Todd, Diana (1998) 'Seismic safety standards for
existing federal buildings', in *Disaster Management
Programs for Historic Sites*, eds Dirk H. R. Spennemann
& David W. Look. San Francisco and Albury: Association for Preservation Technology (Western Chapter) and
The Johnstone Centre, Charles Sturt University. Pp. 63-
64.

11
Seismic safety standards for existing federal buildings

DIANA TODD [¶]

Work by the Interagency Committee on Seismic Safety in Construction is expected to lead
to the eventual development of a systematic program of seismic upgrading for federally
owned or leased buildings. Executive Order 12941, signed on 1 December 1994,
implements a modest program of upgrading the seismic safety of federally owned buildings
and lays the groundwork for developing a more aggressive program, by requiring agencies
to develop a seismic inventory of their existing buildings and an estimate of the cost of
achieving adequate seismic safety in their buildings.

Technical standards

In February 1994, the Interagency Committee on Seismic Safety in Construction issued
Standards of Seismic Safety for Existing Federally Owned or Leased Buildings (RP4). In
addition to specifying appropriate seismic evaluation methodologies, the standard includes
specific items that 'trigger' (necessitate) a seismic evaluation:

- significant remodeling;

- repair of structural damage;

- change of function;

- designation by the owning agency as an 'exceptionally high risk'; and

- newly added to the federal inventory, such as by purchase of donation.

[¶] Building and Fire Research Laboratory, National Institute of Standards & Technology, US Department of
Commerce, Gaithersburg, Maryland, USA

Section 1 of Executive Order 12941 adopts the RP4 standards as the minimum technical criteria that all Executive Branch agencies and departments must meet in future seismic evaluation and mitigation projects. By adopting the RP4 standards, the 'triggers' become mandatory, thus initiating a modest program of seismic evaluation and rehabilitation in all federal agencies. Because the triggers are generally tied to significant changes to a building, the required seismic work takes place during an economically advantageous phase of the building's existence.

The RP4 standards specify life safety as the minimum level of seismic performance to be achieved in 'triggered' buildings. Historic buildings are to be held to the same standard. The Secretary of the Department of the Interior's Standards on Historic Preservation are to be followed in achieving adequate seismic safety.

Collecting information to develop a more active program

Section 2 of Executive Order 12941 requires that all agencies and departments owning or leasing buildings develop a seismic inventory and estimate the costs of mitigating unacceptable seismic risks. The order directs the Interagency Committee on Seismic Safety in Construction to issue, by 1 December 1995, guidance on performing these tasks. The Interagency Committee on Seismic Safety in Construction guidance is expected to call for the inventory to screen buildings into exempt (as defined by RP4) and non-exempt buildings. For non-exempt buildings, information on location (seismicity), occupancy (use), date of construction, model building type, size and number of stories is to be collected. In addition, agencies are asked to indicate whether each building is historic and whether it is considered 'essential' (requires performance above the minimum RP4 life safety level).

The Interagency Committee on Seismic Safety in Construction guidance is expected to recommend that agencies evaluate the seismic safety of all buildings they identify as posing an exceptionally high risk (based on expected frequency and intensity of earthquake occurrence and expected consequences of the event, considering number of occupants, criticality of building function and vulnerability of the structural system). Agencies are asked to evaluate the safety of a representative sample of the remaining non-exempt buildings. For buildings found to be seismically deficient, an estimate of the cost of achieving adequate safety will be required. One source that agencies may use in developing these estimates is Typical Costs For Seismic Rehabilitation, second edition (FEMA 156). That study of over 2,000 seismically rehabilitated buildings found that average costs for rehabilitating historic buildings were nearly three times the average costs for non-historic buildings.

The inventory and cost information is to be forwarded to FEMA by 1 December 1998. FEMA will use the data to examine the costs and benefits of a wide variety of potential programs to upgrade the seismic safety of existing federal buildings. By 1 December 2000, FEMA will submit to Congress the results of their findings. It is hoped that this effort will lead to the adoption of a proactive program of systematic upgrading of the seismic safety of federal buildings.

Morelli, Ugo (1998) 'Seismic safety of existing buildings', in *Disaster Management Programs for Historic Sites*, eds Dirk H. R. Spennemann & David W. Look. San Francisco and Albury: Association for Preservation Technology (Western Chapter) and The Johnstone Centre, Charles Sturt University. Pp. 65-67.

12
Seismic safety of existing buildings

UGO MORELLI [¶]

Since 1984, the Federal Emergency Management Agency (FEMA) has had underway a comprehensive, closely coordinated program to develop a body of building practices that would increase the ability of existing buildings to withstand the forces of earthquakes. Societal implications and issues related to the use of these improved practices have also been examined. At a cost of about US$20 million, two dozen publications, software programs and audio-visual training materials have already been produced and distributed. The intended audience includes design professionals, buildings regulatory personnel, local and state planning and development personnel, high-level managers, master builders, educators, researchers and the general public. The program has proceeded along separate, but parallel, approaches in dealing with private-sector and with federal buildings.

Private-sector buildings

Already available to private-sector practitioners and other interested parties is a 'technical platform' of consensus criteria on how to deal with some of the major engineering aspects of seismic rehabilitation of buildings. This technical material is contained in a trilogy, with supporting documentation, completed in 1989:

- a method for rapid identification of buildings that might be hazardous in case of an earthquake that can be conducted without gaining access to the buildings themselves;

[¶] Policy Manager, Earthquake Program, Federal Emergency Management Agency, 500 C Street, SW, Washington, DC 20472, USA

- a methodology for a more detailed evaluation of a building that identifies structural flaws that have caused collapse in past earthquakes and might do so again in future earthquakes; and

- a compendium of the most commonly used techniques of seismic rehabilitation.

In addition to these engineering topics, the program has also been concerned with societal implications of seismic rehabilitation. In addition to two editions of a study of seismic rehabilitation costs, it has also developed benefit/cost models and associated software for application to both private-sector buildings and federal buildings. For the use of decision makers, major socio-economic issues that are likely to arise in a locality that undertakes seismic rehabilitation of its building stock have been identified, together with ways to array them, and methods to analyze them.

The culminating activity in this field will be the completion in late 1997 of the Guidelines for Seismic Rehabilitation of Buildings and Commentary, a comprehensive set of nationally applicable and consensus-backed technical criteria intended to ensure that buildings will better withstand earthquakes. This is a multi-year, multi-million dollar effort that represents a first of its kind in the United States and will fill a significant gap in the segment of the National Earthquake Hazards Reduction Program dealing with the seismic safety of existing buildings. These publications will allow practitioners to choose design approaches consistent with different levels of seismic safety as required by geographic location, performance objective, type of building, occupancy, or other relevant considerations. Included will be analytical techniques that will yield reliable estimates of the seismic performance of rehabilitated buildings.

Before being issued, the two documents will be given consensus review by representatives of a broad spectrum of users, including the construction industry; building regulatory organizations; building owners and occupants groups; academic and research institutions; financial establishments; local, state and federal levels of government; and the general public. This process is intended to ensure their national applicability and encourage their widespread acceptance and use by practitioners. It is expected that, with time, this set of guidelines will be adapted and adopted by model building code organizations and standards-setting groups, and thus will diffuse widely into the building practices of the United States.

Significant corollary products of this activity are expected. Principal among them will be an engineering applications handbook with refined costs data; a somewhat similar handbook for the use of decision makers at the local government level; a plan for a structured transfer of the technology embodied in the Guidelines using advanced dissemination media; and an identification of the most urgent research and development needs.

Federal buildings

In compliance with a US Congressional mandate contained in Public Law 101-614, a set of technical criteria with commentary was developed by the Interagency Committee on Seismic Safety in Construction, with management and funding by FEMA. The criteria provide federal agencies with minimum life safety standards for both the seismic evaluation and the seismic rehabilitation of buildings in their inventories.   To promulgate the standards, an Executive Order was also prepared.

The Order (No. 12941) was signed by the President on 1 December 1994.   In addition to promulgation of the standards, it initiates a modest program of seismic rehabilitation in Executive Branch owned and leased buildings by requiring that the new standards must be applied in five specified conditions, or 'triggers'.   One such condition, and probably the most significant of the five, is a normal upgrading or rehabilitation of a federally owned or leased building costing more than 50% of the replacement value of that building.   The Order also requires federal agencies to maintain an inventory of their owned and leased building stock and develop data on the cost of seismically rehabilitating it.   These data will be the basis for the preparation by FEMA of a comprehensive long-term program to ensure the seismic safety of all owned and leased federal buildings that is due to the US Congress by 1 December 2000.

Guidance to the agencies as to how to proceed in the preparation of the required materials is under preparation by the Interagency Committee on Seismic Safety in Construction.

Mackensen, Robert (1998) 'Cultural heritage man-
agement and California's State Historical Building Code',
in *Disaster Management Programs for Historic Sites*, eds
Dirk H. R. Spennemann & David W. Look. San
Francisco and Albury: Association for Preservation
Technology (Western Chapter) and The Johnstone
Centre, Charles Sturt University. Pp. 69-73.

13

Cultural heritage management and California's State Historical Building Code

ROBERT MACKENSEN [¶]

California, like many other places, lives under the curse of frequent, sometimes devastating earthquakes. Yet because of that curse, Californians are now blessed with the world's best survivability statistics. In other words, the ratio of lost lives to the severity of the earthquake, as measured by property damage, is the world's lowest. California's building industry and its retrofit programs are essentially doing things right.

Gratefully, for Californians, the biggest post-earthquake problem is not burying its dead but, rather, returning the state to normalcy: recovery. However, the all-too-common practice of jurisdictions seizing on necessary repair work following a disaster as an opportunity to demand *additional* upgrading of routine code non-compliance work, cripples that recovery. Firstly, and however theoretically desirable, such demands add unnecessary costs to an owner already financially and emotionally damaged by the disaster.

The Secretary of the Interior's Standards and the impact of pre- and post-disaster demands on cultural resources

We in California can call on two important tools in order to sensitively and cost-effectively implement historic preservation. 'The Secretary of the Interior's Standards for Rehabilitation' is a universally accepted model for safeguarding the honesty and the integrity of a historic resource. The Secretary's Standards *must be met* if a project:

[¶] State Historic Building Safety Board, 1300 I Street, Suite 800, Sacramento, California 95814, USA. E-mail: RMACKE@smtplink.dsa.ca.gov

- is owned or funded - even in part - by the federal government;

- is owned or funded - even in part - by the State of California;

- is undertaken in any jurisdiction with a local preservation ordinance requiring adherence to the 'Standards'; or

- is to receive preservation investment tax credits.

The second tool is California's State Historical Building Code. It is the vehicle which makes meeting the Standards both feasible and cost-effective. By statute, it governs all other statutes and regulations as they may apply to historic resources within the State. The State Historical Building Code empowers owners and jurisdictions to minimize alterations and modifications, and to ensure that they are sensitive to the historic resource rather than intrusive. Essentially, the State Historical Building Code looks on historic resources as though they are ongoing occupancies, subject - naturally - to 'health and safety' issues, but unconcerned with routine non-compliance issues, just as are all other ongoing occupancies in a community's building stock. Thus, the State Historical Building Code contains no 'triggers', nor does it recognize 'triggers' found in other codes. Rather, it is a mandate, by means of adopting reasonable alternatives and reasonable levels of equivalency, to ensure the continued viability of our historic resources.

Historic preservation, distilled to its basics, is composed of two elements: *Honesty* and *Commitment*. Honesty is about the resource and the commitment is to pass these historic buildings and sites onto the next generation as unaltered as possible. We cannot let ourselves lose sight of these basics. The State Historical Building Code and the Secretary of the Interior's Standards for Rehabilitation facilitate that honesty and commitment. However, even as we make the changes necessary to ensure the continued viability of these buildings and sites, we must never forget that, just like with vintage cars, every alteration diminishes the ability to accurately convey - or understand - our history.

Seismic safety of existing federal buildings

The federal Standards of Seismic Safety for Existing Federally Owned or Leased Buildings (RP4) are being applied equally to non-historic and historic buildings. This policy runs the risk of imposing an unnecessary burden on those resources which society has determined worthy of preservation. A better call might be the one made by the chief of one of California's most important life safety agencies when a number of such concerns brought us all together at Hearst Castle at San Simeon: "When it comes to historic resources", he told the assembled officials, "we should simply close the code books and start using knowledge, experience, and common sense". Since the 1970s, that has been the advice of Section 104(f) of the Uniform Building Code which - paraphrased - says that the end result of work on historic resources may not be more hazardous to the public health, safety and welfare than the building's condition before rehabilitation work started.

How is that for a call for flexibility? Without sacrificing life safety considerations - which must always be paramount - California's State Historical Building Code simply builds on the premise of Section 104(f). It is, in fact, a mandate to implement reasonable alternatives whenever a structure's historic fabric or historic character is threatened by the language of the community's regular codes and ordinances.

The State Historical Building Code is a performance code. As such, sometimes its enforcement options vary widely and disputes arise as to reasonable alternatives. Sometimes, disputed issues must be settled by the final administrative authority a statutory established 21-member State Historical Building Safety Board - which is the final administrative authority. However, it is interesting to note that attempts are underway to convert both structural codes and fire codes to 'performance' documents, recognizing that mega-structures like large exhibition centers simply no longer can be built under the prescriptive values found in existing codes.

Like these mega-structures, the only way to successfully deal with the unique character of historic resources is to recognize their special qualities; then to agree to protect these qualities by making the commitment to impose no rigid repair and/or upgrade standards. Only then can come the freedom and latitude to generate the best possible combination of intrusion and sensitivity for the achievement of life and property protection.

Thanks in no small measure to the State Historical Building Code, California's major cultural icons continue to give valuable service while retaining their historic integrity. The Los Angeles Coliseum, San Francisco's City Hall and Ferry Building, the California Missions and a host of others, are all able to continue to accurately reflect their past while preparing themselves for the future.

The roles of other federal, state and local agencies and commissions

As has been said so many times: *Before* the earthquake, "tie it down and tie it together!". Between Loma Prieta and Northridge, the International Conference of Building Officials produced a 20-minute video entitled 'Bolt it Down'. It is designed for home owners, do-it-yourselfers, and it is very good. It is particularly valuable because it addresses the seismic upgrading in a setting separate from the trauma of post-disaster repair and recovery.

The post-earthquake imposition of substantial mandatory programs for seismically upgrading the existing stock of buildings - particularly when imposed as a condition of repair and occupancy of an already damaged structure - could well create a financial burden beyond the owner's capabilities, and thus pose a threat to the continued existence of these buildings. For historic resources, whose protection and preservation is in the public interest, this is not an acceptable situation.

The 'safe' or 'earthquake-proof' building is essentially non-existent. All our codes and ordinances can really provide is a degree of defense from risk that society agrees is reasonable. The annual loss of life from lightning is clear evidence that even innocently occupying open space is not risk-free. Moreover, society has endorsed a whole hierarchy of levels of risk, and presumably considers them all 'reasonable'. Does the fact that Californian schools are designed to more rigid standards mean that Californian hotels are not 'safe'? Everything we inhabit - structures, ships, automobiles and aircraft - involves a cost-benefit ratio in which is a risk factor. That some people choose not to fly, while others refuse to ride in a sub-compact car, does not negate the 'public good' that these means of travel engender.

The same applies to historic buildings. Within commonly accepted standards of 'reasonable protection', it is in the public interest to retain and protect our cultural heritage. The Uniform Building Code, Section 104(f), has been facilitating this protection since the 1970s. California's State Historical Building Code simply elaborates on this theme, calling for alternative solutions, listing some and leaving the remainder to the knowledge, experience and judgment of officials, most of whom recognize that the mandates for health and safety *and* for preservation are *both* important threads of a common legal fabric of the people's thinking.

Yet there is a disturbing change in perspective looming on the horizon: the removal from California of any differentiation of seismic zones for code enforcement purposes. The result is likely to be a 'one-size-fits-all' approach to seismic retrofit. Strangely, this is occurring just when the level of technical expertise is more and more able to determine locations and maximum credible strengths of earthquakes in California.

The seismic upgrading of historic resources, in order to be both adequate and sensitive, cannot abandon the necessity for resolution on a case-by-case basis. The imposition of a 'one-size-fits-all' or a 'cook book' solution would likely put our cultural heritage as much at risk from the 'solution' as from the 'problem'. No one argues extraordinary and case-specific measures to protect and conserve the historic treasures of a museum. The cultural legacy of our historic buildings is worthy of equal consideration.

The State Historical Building Code provides Californians with the legal framework to uniquely tailor whatever work is necessary to the individual needs of the historic resource. For jurisdictions to impose 'cookbook' solutions, depriving these resources of reasonable, sensitive and cost-effective alternatives could, indeed, constitute a 'taking'.

Effects of current FEMA policies and code enforcement

Subsequent to California's Loma Prieta Earthquake, the citizens passed a bond issue for the seismic retrofit of local structures housing essential services, and of a number of major state-owned buildings. Among the policies established for state-owned buildings was that if retrofit costs exceeded 60% of the cost of new construction, demolition becomes an option. However, for historic resources, only when retrofit costs exceed 120% of the cost of new construction, does demolition become an option.

With this distinction, the State has recognized a fundamental difference between the value placed on the two types of structures. Most of the federal government also genuinely acknowledges the profound difference between standard buildings and those which have become an element of our cultural legacy, and Section 106 of the National Historic Preservation Act underscores that fact. Yet federal RP4 standards for seismic upgrading impose the same demands on non-historic and historic buildings, thereby generating sometimes unnecessarily intrusive solutions. There is a need to amend these standards, recognizing that the protection of our historic resources deserves special consideration while concurrently ensuring a reasonable level of life safety. This is particularly important for the continuing viability of federal buildings in California.

Post-earthquake repair and structural upgrading of California's historic resources have generated a great deal of discussion regarding the appropriate degree of intrusiveness of the work, *vis-a-vis* the latitude available under California's State Historical Building Code. While some owners may be guilty of looking for a way for the government to pick up the costs for not only repair, but for decades of deferred maintenance, some members of those government agencies may be equally in error for looking for ways to merely 'paint the cracks'. Neither approach is right.

It must be recognized, that while the State Historical Building Code is a call for making the least intrusive modifications necessary to retain the viability of California's historic resources, a justifiable case can readily be made that, when addressing seismic stability, this is not a call for the barest minimum of work, but rather a call for the most prudent balance of intrusion and preservation that will effect the highest reasonable level of protection against future significant damage or loss of the historic resource.

Perhaps we need a sliding 'cost multiplier' to better reflect these values - '1' reflecting a non-historic building, and up to '10' reflecting, say, the Lincoln Memorial. I have little doubt that this nation's citizens, in order to repair, restore and preserve that hallowed structure, would gladly spend ten times the cost of a replacement stucco box of the same dimensions.

I would like to suggest that the National Park Service and FEMA, along with California's Office of Emergency Services and the State Historic Preservation Office, investigate and adopt a hierarchy of such values to be assigned to California's historic resources. If accomplished prior to a disaster, it could provide a rational basis for assigning premium repair dollars for those icons of our society whose loss would be unthinkable, and are therefore deserving of upgraded (and consequently more costly) levels of protection.

It is not much different than Homeowner's Insurance. With good reason, we rarely are willing to insure for nothing more than the depreciated value of used goods. Rather, we highly value our homes and their contents. They tell us who we are. No-one even questions the appropriateness of full replacement value insurance. Historic buildings tell a community - or a nation - who and what we are. This heritage is no less deserving of the same special consideration.

Langenbach, Randolph (1998) 'Architectural issues in the seismic rehabilitation of masonry buildings', in *Disaster Management Programs for Historic Sites*, eds Dirk H. R. Spennemann & David W. Look. San Francisco and Albury: Association for Preservation Technology (Western Chapter) and The Johnstone Centre, Charles Sturt University. Pp. 75-90.

14

Architectural issues in the seismic rehabilitation of masonry buildings

RANDOLPH LANGENBACH [¶]

Our approach to the structure of buildings has gone through a transformation in modern times. Traditionally, most major buildings were solid walled structures with the walls bearing directly on the ground. With the current predominance of steel and reinforced concrete as the materials of choice for larger buildings, we are now used to the erection of frames, onto which the enclosure cladding system is attached.

With the 'post-modern' fascination with historical forms and details, the contrast between the old and new systems has only recently become particularly noticeable. This style shift has brought back a desire to design buildings which have the solid walls of their historic counterparts, but which, unlike them, have to be constructed as a series of light, jointed panels attached to the underlying frame. Often the results simply fail to capture the kind of texture and meaning which is found in the older buildings. Architects continue to struggle for solutions, only to find that the source of the feeling they are trying to capture is simply not accessible in Dryvit, GFRC, Fiberglas, or panelized veneer brick, with their frequent need for expansion joints cutting across the architectural details. As engineers work hard to convert the highly indeterminate, ambiguous and nonlinear behavior of historic masonry construction into something which can be understood with mathematical certainty, architects struggle to wrest control of the seemingly rigid and unyielding materials of modern day conventional building systems, trying to breathe the kind of subtle life into them that they find at the root of the aesthetic quality of historic structures.

[¶] Senior Analyst and Historic Building Specialist, Federal Emergency Management Agency, 500 C Street, SW, Room 713, Washington, DC 20007, USA. E-mail: LONGBROOK@aol.com

This transformation in construction technology parallels a similar change in engineering practice which now relies to a great extent on frame analysis for the design of building structures. Traditional heavy wall masonry buildings tend to defy analysis by the usual present day methods, forcing many practicing professionals to do what they do not like to do - designing in part by guess work. Research in the area of unreinforced masonry is so important because without it, historical buildings will be lost simply because engineers and architects will be loath to touch them because they cannot be made to fit their mathematical design models. This may be true even though the same structures have withstood major past earthquakes, and the damage record is known. For example, a number of historic buildings in California which survived the 1906 San Francisco Earthquake are threatened now more by hazard mitigation legislation than by future earthquakes.

The cultural significance of historic building fabric

Modern engineering science, new materials and current codes have gone a long way towards reducing the fear of catastrophe and death from earthquakes. This has been true despite the spectacular failures which each major earthquake seems to leave in its wake. Earthquake design is an evolving and constantly changing practice largely because the actual events are so rare, and when they do occur, the earthquake forces can be so large that some structural damage is expected even in new structures. As a result, the line between acceptable and unacceptable risk and performance is vague and fluid.

In the field of historic preservation, the problem of seismic risk cannot be solved by stricter design codes, better new materials, or a more stringent engineering design. It is exactly these things which heighten the dilemma with older structures, threatening the very historical qualities which we seek to save.

It has become a familiar sight in many parts of the world to see the stone exterior walls of gutted buildings held up by shoring while they await the construction of new interior floors and roof. Fine old masonry buildings are often stripped of their interior finishes, with the steel reinforcing rods being erected against the inside of the exterior walls in preparation for a sheet of concrete. Roofs of ancient tiles or slate are torn off to be replaced by new tiles and slate after the obligatory concrete or plywood diaphragm is installed.

One might ask "what's the fuss - the exterior walls have been preserved, have they not? The interior will be rebuilt and the new work will be hidden - the view will be just the same when it is all completed". Many architects, not just engineers, fail to understand the meaning of what is lost along the way when this kind of work is carried out. Donald Appleyard observed:

> The professional and scientific view of the environment usually suppresses its meaning.... Environmental professionals have not been aware of the symbolic content of the environment, or of the symbolic nature of their own plans and projects.... Professionals see the environment as a physical entity, a functional container,...a setting for social action or programs, a pattern of land uses, a sensuous experience - but seldom as a social or political symbol (Appleyard 1978).

Figure 14.1. This building in Kashmir illustrates the combined timber and masonry construction which was developed to resist the earthquakes which frequently affected this soft soil lakeside site. The timbers only run horizontally, but they serve to tie the masonry construction together.

Historic buildings do not just carry their cultural significance as relics by image alone. While understanding the architectural style and decorative form of historic structures is important, the cultural meaning of many of the most significant buildings is resident within the reality of the artifact itself. A historic structure is important because it is exactly that - it is old, and thus has been a part of human lives. As the English critic John Ruskin eloquently stated:

> Indeed the greatest glory of a building is not in its stones, or in its gold. Its glory is in its Age, and in that deep sense of voicefulness, of stern watching, of mysterious sympathy, nay, even of approval or condemnation, which we feel in walls that have long been washed by the passing waves of humanity....

> It is in that golden stain of time that we are to look for the real light, and color, and preciousness of architecture; and it is not until a building has assumed this character, till it has been entrusted with the fame, and hallowed by the deeds of men, till its walls have been witnesses of suffering, and its pillars rise out of the shadows of death, that its existence, more lasting as it is than that of the natural objects of the world around it, can be gifted with even so much as these possess of language and of life (Ruskin 1901).

Seismic protection and strengthening forces us to confront one of the central dilemmas of historic preservation - the fact that preservation is forced to encompass change and renewal. Unlike maintenance and rehabilitation from decay, a seismic project may tear apart a building which was otherwise in good repair and make it almost entirely new. In such an instance, only the image, rather than the substance, of much of the historic fabric is preserved. Masonry buildings are particularly vulnerable to this approach.

Sometimes seismic projects are promoted as opportunities to 'restore' the original appearance of a buildings, stripping away the later alterations in order to return them to their original appearance. In Sacramento, California, the State Capitol is such an example. The Capitol was completely gutted in 1976, leaving only the exterior walls and the central drum and dome. All of the interior floors and walls were removed and replaced in reinforced concrete. The remaining masonry was covered with an internal skin of shotcrete and the floors were replaced in reinforced concrete. As a result, while the interior of this building is now genuinely spectacular, with impressive museum rooms, excellent craftsmanship, rich materials, stunning colors and textures, none of it is genuine. A 'heart transplant' was authorized when an 'ace bandage' may have been all that was needed. The Capitol needed to be strengthened and repaired, but one should ask whether the risk identified in 1971 could not have been satisfactorily alleviated by less drastic, destructive, and expensive measures.

> The quest for authenticity, and the search for 'real' meaning through 'honesty' of form, often leads to the destruction of that which it seeks by inducing fakery....Authenticity is not a property of environmental form, but of process and relationship....Authentic meaning cannot be created through the manipulation or purification of form, since authenticity is the very source from which form gains meaning (Seamon & Mugerauer 1985).

This gutting of structures for seismic strengthening is not limited to the United States. For example, following the 1979 earthquake in Montenegro, Yugoslavia, many structures in the historic city of Kotor have been reconstructed with reinforced concrete floors, replacing the original heavy timber. In some of these structures, reinforced concrete columns have been cut into the masonry, forming completely new reinforced concrete structures, with the historic masonry reduced to a veneer.

Another example, in Portugal, is the little mountain village of Piódau.   The Portuguese government recently listed this picturesque mountain village of stone buildings as a historical site.   Located in earthquake-prone country, many of the stone houses are being strengthened.   The typical seismic strengthening consists of replacing their timber floor and roof structures with reinforced concrete.   Some of the walls, which had been laid with very little mortar, are being re-laid in strong cement mortar.   While undoubtedly safer, the visual effect of this work is the loss of the texture and feel of the traditional surfaces.   The patina and sense of the country masons' and plasterers' handiwork is erased.   If the approach had been to repair and augment the timber interior structures and tie them to the existing walls, rather than replace them, the historical quality of the buildings would have survived the life safety improvements.

The debate over such alternatives always turns to the question of how much life safety protection is enough.   When existing archaic construction remains in use, even if improved, can it be relied on to perform adequately? However, at the core of this issue is the fact that, unless the architects, planners and engineers identify and understand the importance of the original structural and interior fabric of the historical buildings, and bring this understanding into their designs, such destruction will continue because they will do what they are used to doing with new structures.   This consideration must include the evidence of the original handiwork, rather than just the appearance of a building from a distance.

Another striking example is South Hall at the University of California, Berkeley. Constructed of brick with timber floors in the 1870s, South Hall is the oldest surviving building on the campus.   In the 1980s, it was gutted to undergo seismic strengthening under the University's campus-wide program. The retrofit plans included the reinforced concrete 'shotcrete' jacketing of the inside surface of many of the exterior walls, and the demolition and replacing of the timber floors with steel and concrete.   In the process of carving channels into the walls, it was discovered that the original builders had installed bond-iron in the masonry - continuous bars of wrought iron which extended from corner to corner above and below the windows in all of the building's walls.   Dog anchors, which secured the floors to the walls, were also discovered hidden in the walls.   At the corners, the bond iron bars were secured by large bosses on gigantic cast iron plates which formed part of the architecture of the building.

Because the designers had never thought to investigate the structural history of the building, including whether these great cast iron ornamental plates on the corners of the building served a structural purpose, the existence of the bond iron was not known until the demolition for the retrofit.   All of these bond iron bars were cut as a result.   In addition, as historically significant and advanced as this original system was, no recordation of its design was ever conducted.   The irony was that one of the engineers said that, had they known of the existence of the bond iron and the dog anchors, their designs may have been different and less extensive.   When it was discovered, however, it was too late to change the designs, and the early seismic technology was destroyed.

Figure 14.2. The photo of the exterior with construction of the front steps shows San Francisco City Hall in December, 1997, during the 4 year long $300 million project to seismically retrofit the building with base isolation. This view shows the rebuilding of the stone front steps with a massive cantilever supporting structure to allow them to sway with the building during an earthquake.

One may ask, "Why is it important to preserve what had been hidden in the historic walls - nobody could see it anyway?" Perhaps documenting it, which was not done, would have been sufficient, but this example also illustrates one of the important points about seismic design - that is that many engineers and architects have the false belief that the today's engineering design is, not only better than anything which has been done in the past, but is the ultimate solution which will require no further interventions. They believe that their work will make the building strong and complete, and that no-one will have to do anything other than maintenance and superficial remodeling ever again. Here, at South Hall, the designers failed to know what had been put into the walls to resist earthquakes a mere 100 years ago, despite the fact that great cast iron plates to which the bond iron straps were attached, were fully exposed on the outside of the building. What is there to make certain that our successors will be any better informed about the work done today?

In addition, with the irreversible conversion of the masonry walls of South Hall into a veneer of masonry on reinforced concrete, the integrity of those walls as masonry walls was destroyed. One of the principal advantages of masonry is that it can be repaired by being dismantled and relaid. Now it has been fused together into one solid mass of unyielding concrete. Years later, it will not be possible to repair the brickwork or replace the concrete jacket because of rusting of the re-bars or for any other reason. The present-day seismic work will indeed last the life of the building simply because the building's life is now forced to be limited to that of the new work.

This point may seem far-fetched, but historical buildings are worthy of such long-term consideration. It should be remembered that the 19th century restorers of the Parthenon introduced iron cramps which, when they rusted in the 20th century, destroyed some of the original marbles. Should anyone wonder whether the state-of-the-art at the time of the 19th century restoration represented progress from earlier times, they should consider the fact that the ancient builders had used a less rust-prone iron, which, when protected by a lead jacket, survived over 2,000 years to this day without distress.

Learning from the past

Many people make the mistake of thinking that it is only our generation which has discovered ways of resisting the threat of earthquakes in structural design. They come to believe that older forms of construction practice must be more dangerous simply because they were designed before current seismic codes were promulgated, or before current engineering knowledge about earthquakes had been developed. Certainly, the introduction of steel provides ductility where masonry could not, and yet the recent discoveries of the failures of the welds in over 100 of the 400 steel buildings affected by the Northridge Earthquake should provide some humility in the face of this awesome force. While many masonry buildings have tumbled in earthquakes, they have not always tumbled. As was witnessed in Armenia recently, it was the modern reinforced concrete buildings which collapsed, killing thousands, while the older masonry buildings nearby remained mostly intact, providing refuge for the displaced occupants of the newer buildings.

In places as diverse as Turkey, Yugoslavia, Kashmir and Nicaragua, indigenous forms of construction were developed or adapted to respond to the earthquake threat where available resources demanded that masonry continue to be used. In Kashmir, an elaborate system of interlocking horizontal timber runner beams was used, without vertical wood columns, to hold the rubble masonry and soft mud mortar buildings together on the silty soil. Historical reports confirm that these buildings withstood earthquakes better than the nearby unreinforced brick palace and British-built government buildings.

Today, many of these vernacular structures are falling in favor of reinforced concrete structures, which, because of poor local construction practices, may actually prove to be less resistant than their 'low tech', unengineered historic predecessors.

Restoration professionals sometimes fail to understand the subtleties of seismic resistance in older structures. Believing that strength and stiffness is necessary, they destroy original construction systems to gain sheer strength at the expense of earlier solutions which may still be valid. In Dubrovnik, before the recent civil war, restorers of the historic palace uncovered an interior wall they had thought was solid masonry to find a basket-weave of small timber studs, with brick or stone masonry loosely fitted together between the studs. The restoration engineer stated at a conference that this "poorly constructed wall was immediately removed and replaced during the restoration of the building". Instead of being 'poorly constructed', this wall deliberately may have been constructed in this fashion to resist earthquakes. The wall, which was similar to Bahareque construction found in Central America, may have represented a far greater understanding of seismic engineering than pre-modern builders are given credit for today.

Building conservation practice *versus* seismic strengthening

While it is impossible to ignore present-day advances and advocate a return to traditional construction practice, the narrow assumption that 'new is always better' can blind us to the potential gains which an understanding of the earlier forms of construction may provide us in the present. This is particularly true for the advancement of building conservation and seismic rehabilitation practice. For years, these have been seen as separate and opposing fields of practice, with solutions which seem in basic conflict with each other. For example, for years, conservation professionals have specified that restoration mortar consist of a high lime mix which is weaker than the masonry units. Code requirements have established that mortar must consist of a high cement mixture and meet high strength standards which have proven to be anathema to proper conservation of older masonry walls. The discovery of the importance of reducing or eliminating Portland cement from masonry mortars in restoration is one of the cornerstones of recent conservation practice:

> The use of lime-sand mortar ... furnishes a plastic cushion that allows bricks or stones some movement relative to each other. The entire structural system depends upon some flexibility in the masonry components of a building. A cushion of soft mortar furnishes sufficient flexibility to compensate for uneven settlement of foundations, walls, piers and arches: gradual adjustment over a period of months or years is possible. In a structure that lacks flexibility, stones and bricks break, mortar joints open and serious damage results (McKee 1980 - tense changed for clarity).

This was not meant to refer to masonry in earthquakes, but in light of the Kashmiri experience it is intriguing to ask, whether the notion of a 'plastic cushion' might be an appropriate concept for walls subjected to earthquake forces. It is worth noting the conflict between the Historic Preservation documents which recommend using the weakest and most lime-rich ASTM formula (K) 1 unit cement to 2.25-4 units lime for restoration work, and the Uniform Building Code, which prohibits the use of mortar weaker than the three strongest categories, known as ASTM types M, S & N: 1 unit cement to 0.25-1.25 units lime) for any mortar used in structural masonry (which includes, of course, most historic masonry walls).

One reason for this conflict is that while the Code is founded upon the performance of the wall under load at its design strength at the point of construction, the preservation documents are aimed towards maximizing the long-term durability of walls with relatively weak masonry units in response to all environmental conditions. One only needs to compare the long-term performance of ancient masonry and modern masonry to see the merits in the softer, high lime mortars, and yet, the codes now make beneficial use of this knowledge difficult. Other examples abound where modern uses of masonry has proven short-lived because of environmental degradation of the system. Seismic design must fit into a larger performance picture, where other environmental assaults are considered as well as the occasional earthquake.

A crisis of cost

Concerns over the impact of seismic strengthening policies is more than just one of potential loss of original fabric; it is also one of economics. As long as politicians and the public believe that historic masonry buildings are enormously risky unless great sums of money are spent to convert their structural systems into steel or concrete, vast numbers of important cultural monuments are at risk. This issue has expanded recently in the United States to include large-scale 20th century masonry buildings constructed with steel or concrete frames. It is exactly the current crisis with these types of buildings which confirm the importance of engineering research and the development of specialized codes for masonry buildings and historic buildings in general.

The crisis can be illustrated by an example in Oakland, California, where one brick- and terracotta-clad steel frame historical building, the City Hall, is being repaired from Loma Prieta Earthquake damage and seismically upgraded at the extraordinary cost of US$530 per square foot (US$5,700/square meter), which is more than three times the cost of a new building of comparable quality. Six blocks away, another office building, the Oakland Medical Building, was just repaired and seismically upgraded to the same codes for a cost of only US$11 per square foot (US$118/square meter). The City Hall design uses the now popular newly developed base isolation technology, while the Medical Building is a fixed base design, but both schemes were promoted as 'cost effective' designs to meet the requirements of the building code (see Figure 14.3).

With a difference between two projects, both promoted as necessary and expedient, of over 35 times, it is evident that there is little consensus in this particular field over what is required and beneficial to meet the seismic threat. While certainly the expected performance of the base isolated design is greater than the fixed base design, and even though part of the difference is for interior remodeling of the City Hall, it is questionable whether this justifies 35 times the cost. While many celebrated the repair and upgrade solution for City Hall because it preserved the building, historic preservation suffers in the long run from such gargantuan projects as that of the Oakland City Hall because the public begins to believe that such costly solutions are the only way to make such buildings safe.

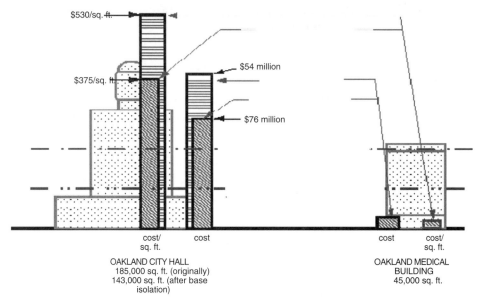

Figure 14.3. Cost comparison between two retrofit projects

The situation with bearing wall masonry buildings in California is no longer as distorted. The reason for this is that recent research has resulted in the development of a new code specific to this building type. While public perception on the safety of masonry buildings is still unduly negative, and price spreads between different engineers' designs can still be large, the existence of this new code has helped to narrow the spread, and make economical solutions possible.

The code for masonry buildings, which has now been adopted as a model code in California is Appendix, Chapter 1 of the Uniform Code for Building Conservation. This appendix contains the engineering provisions for bearing wall masonry structures. These provisions were derived from the 'ABK Methodology', an engineering design methodology for unreinforced masonry bearing wall buildings developed by a team of engineers in Los Angeles under a research grant from the National Science Foundation.

One of the principal features of this methodology is the provisions which anticipate and exploit the post-elastic behavior of the wood and plaster interior partitions and floor diaphragms, thus computing a consequential reduction in the forces on the masonry walls. Another result of the ABK research is the finding that masonry buildings actually respond differently from the way the traditional codes and engineering approaches assumed. Rather than amplifying the forces of the earthquake, the heavy masonry-walled building has the effect of dampening the shaking by acting as a "rigid rocking block on a soft soil base". This is to be compared with the common code analysis of seismic force on a building which models the building as a "single degree of freedom, 5% damped elastic oscillator with a fixed base" (Kariotis *et al.* 1984; Kariotis, J. 1989, pers. comm., 3 June).

Figure 14.4. The photo of the interior structure is of the Oakland City Hall during the approximately $80 million retrofit project to base isolate the building. The photograph shows the steel frame with brick masonry infill construction, and also shows the typical hollow clay interior partition construction on the left.

Using the ABK method of analysis, the computed force levels in an unreinforced masonry building are lower than found under conventional code analysis. The results of this methodology on the design of retrofit strategies for individual masonry buildings is that the amount of strengthening work which is computed to be required is less than that shown as needed when conventional strength based linear elastic analysis is used. This approach thus reduces the retrofit intervention and costs.

An even more significant step for historical buildings in general has been taken in California with the adoption of the State Historical Building Code. This Code, which applies to all historical buildings, including even those which are only on local lists, allows much greater design and engineering flexibility than is possible under the conventional prevailing code which is primarily meant for new buildings.

Instead of prescriptive requirements, the State Historical Building Code describes general performance objectives which must be met. The specific solutions are left up to the designers. The code also encourages the use of archaic materials and systems as part of the structural system, providing some minimum values for these systems where they are available.

Areas for further research and development

Engineering research

Three topics for further research which would benefit masonry building preservation particularly come to mind. One is the study of the effects of mortars of varying strength and constituents, a second is further study to develop code values for stone masonry, particularly with a random ashlar or rubble wall bedding pattern, and a third is further study on the post-elastic in-plane strength and behavior of masonry bearing and infill walls.

Mortar

Most masonry wall studies have not introduced mortar strength and mortar ingredients as the principal variable in laboratory experiments. The potential benefits of high lime mortar in construction are well known in the field of building conservation technology, but not adequately explored in terms of its effects on seismic performance. Historic walls are often treated only as dead load in lateral capacity analysis because of low mortar strength, but when combined with certain bedding plane and window-frame reinforcing techniques, the performance of such walls may be made satisfactory by restraining deformations and avoiding collapse potential, while allowing for cracking and energy dissipation. The objectives of such research would be to establish a sound basis for the preservation of the integrity of historic stone and brick masonry by avoiding the need for destructive concrete coatings.

The most important attribute of mortar strengths below that of the masonry units is that, when the wall does crack, it does so along the mortar joints. This results in greater overall stability than if the units themselves were to fracture. At the 1988 International Brick/Block Masonry Conference in Dublin, a paper by Dr. W. Mann, University of Darmstadt, generated criticism around the assertion that masonry bedded in mortar with "low cohesion [is] favorable" because it contributes to a type of "ductile" behavior.

Such a statement is diametrically opposed to the conventional wisdom that mortar must be strong to resist earthquakes. However, in the traditional examples described above, where the weak mortar is combined with the overall flexibility of the building structure, the restraint provided by the timber beams, and the pre-compression provided by the weight of the overburden, weak mortar may be more resistant to catastrophic fracture and collapse by allowing the cracks to be distributed throughout the wall. The flexibility and internal damping of the structure can serve to change the building's response, reducing the out-of-plane forces in the masonry walls while the timber serves to keep the weaker masonry in place. While research has shown that weak mortar can cause problems with unreinforced masonry walls, particularly for out-of-plane shaking, perhaps some mechanical ties within the walls can fill the role that the timbers did in traditional construction by holding the masonry units in place while the wall deforms.

There has been some significant progress in this direction in Europe, and even in New Zealand. In Greece and New Zealand, several projects have achieved seismic strengthening by simply wrapping cables around the masonry structure, which are hidden by the stucco, or left visible on the surface. Utilizing the strengthening effect caused by tying the masonry together to create horizontal bands similar in their purpose to the timber runners of the Dhajji-Dwari system, these buildings continue to bear their own weight on the unaltered existing masonry. Such systems have the advantage of causing little disruption to the historic masonry surface or the integrity of the wall. The cables are also accessible for inspection and can easily be replaced. What is radical about this and other surface-mounted strengthening systems is that the retrofit work is left visible as a frank statement of this part of the building's historical evolution. Sometimes it is important to recognize that, as was the case with South Hall, greater damage may be incurred by making changes hidden behind walls which have been radically altered or rebuilt, than by exposing the changes in front of walls which are thus left intact.

Stone masonry.ii.stone masonry; code values .ii.Building materials:stone masonry;

There is a need for more information on capacity values for rubble and random ashlar masonry which can be introduced into the building codes. Engineers are loath to apply the values which have been developed for brick masonry, but the recommended test techniques, such as the push test, are only remotely applicable to stone masonry situations. Lacking even minimum code capacity values, the conservative approach is to impart little or no capacity to the existing masonry. In the United States, this has resulted in costly and invasive designs for many stone buildings and the unnecessary demolition of a number of important historical buildings because retrofit schemes proposed proved to be too expensive.

Post-elastic behavior

More research is also needed on the post-elastic behavior of masonry of all types. Even the recent unreinforced masonry building codes developed in California stop short of including values derived from the behavior of masonry when it is cracking and yielding in an earthquake. The codes for present-day construction such as steel and reinforced concrete are based on linear elastic calculations using reduced forces to approximate post-elastic actual behavior, but designers often give very low values to masonry because of its lack of material ductility. However, as a system, there is substantial remaining capacity in a wall which has begun to crack before it becomes unstable. If buildings fell down the moment masonry walls exceeded their elastic strength, there would have been far greater death and destruction in past earthquakes. Practicing engineers are often loath to depend on masonry for part of the load-resisting mechanism because of the lack of realistic code values on which to base their design, and thus protect their liability in the event that an earthquake exceeds the strength of the wall.

Building codes

The adoption of the Uniform Code for Building Conservation as a State of California's model code for existing buildings, and the enactment of the State of California Historical Building Code have both gone a long way to allowing for sensitive and cost effective improvements to historical buildings in California. A code specific to the masonry infill frame building type is under development by a team of California engineers. The absence of such a code has been made conspicuous by the breadth of costs between different projects, and the sometimes acrimonious disagreements over what strengthening is necessary.

In Europe, as the European Community has moved towards unified building codes, the problem of making existing buildings, particularly historical buildings in different countries, fit into the a single universal code must be dealt with. It is strongly recommended that a separate code for historical buildings be developed. Like the State Historical Building Code in California, this code should be based on performance objectives, rather than prescriptive construction procedures or systems. An Internationally standard code which applies to new and old buildings alike, will fail to cover the specific needs of historical building types which vary from region to region. What may be sound practice in one area, may be destructive of cultural value in another. Provisions for existing buildings with archaic construction systems and earlier interior layouts, must be included into alternate codes or many buildings will be lost.

Engineer's liability

A discussion of codes inevitably leads to a discussion of the problems surrounding professional liability. In the United States, many preservation problems result from the fact that engineers and architects are afraid of malpractice claims if they undertake solutions which are different from the code, and if damage occurs in an earthquake. This has often forced them to be more conservative with existing masonry buildings than they would have to be with new buildings. This is true because the code for new buildings, although expecting structural damage to occur in a major earthquake, is very specific in the construction requirements. With old buildings with archaic pre-code structural systems which cannot be made to meet the letter of the current code, designers feel vulnerable to lawsuits regardless of the level of damage.

In a sense, present-day professionals thus feel forced to take responsibility for the performance of the existing building structures designed by others before their time, when all they have been hired to do is to provide some improvement to them. As a result, the owner's desire for the most minimal upgrade often balloons into a major expensive project, with hundreds or thousands of pages of engineering analysis and justification. For every project of this kind which is constructed, hundreds of buildings remain without any improvements because of the severe cost and liability implications if they are touched at all.

Life safety

Finally, a discussion of appropriate codes, professional liability and even topics for scientific research must include also a discussion and resolution of what level of seismic protection is necessary. Codes serve to establish a lower bound of performance, but they are not designed to provide guidance as to what should be the upper bound. Economic forces are expected to provide this, but in the field of seismic upgrading, particularly for large public projects involving government funds, confusion over how much is enough has prevented people from reaching consensus on this issue. This has been true largely because the issue of life safety is so unclear. It is as laudable as a goal as it is vague as a benchmark. For example, while modern building codes assume structural damage may occur to a code-conforming new building in the event of an earthquake, many engineers and architects are loath to define what is acceptable damage for historic masonry buildings, resulting in vast expenses for new supporting structural systems. What had been acceptable only fifty years ago, is now suddenly unacceptable. In the case of frame-and-infill masonry buildings, provisions are sometimes even made to resist the potential of collapse in building types which have not had a history of collapsing in earthquakes in the past.

Conclusion

Historic structures have something to tell us which transcends their formal architectural language. This gift from the past can be erased if the integrity of the original structure is destroyed to meet the demands of hazard mitigation. Understanding both the positive and the negative attributes of masonry construction can guide us towards methods which may be less destructive of original fabric. Some of these methods may even be more effective over the long-term, not only because they build on strengths which already exist, but also because they are more closely derived from local, social and economic conditions. The purpose of historic preservation is not limited to the static freezing of artifacts. It also has to do with preserving continuity within the slow evolution of building traditions - a continuity which may in the end provide the most effective and lasting defense against earthquakes.

Regardless of whether a masonry building is modeled by an engineer as a 'rigid block on soil springs', or as a 'non-ductile, rigid mass on a fixed base', in truth it has life. It moves, it changes color, it ages and it responds to our own images and dreams of what buildings should be. By 'moves', this is not intended to mean falling down in an earthquake, but rather the slow and subtle movement over time - by the heat of the day - by the gradual settlement of the foundations - or by the slow erosion of the mortar bed or of the bricks or stones themselves. This almost organic quality is essential to the aesthetic quality of historic masonry. If we could arrest the effects of time, traditional masonry might lose its magic. Even in earthquake country, it is this essential quality of building which must be preserved.

Bibliography

Appelyard, D. (1978) The Environment as a Social Symbol: Towards a Theory of Environmental Action and Perception, Berkeley Institute of Urban and Regional Development, UC, Berkeley, unpub.

Kariotis, J. *et al.* n (1984) 'ABK Methodology for the Mitigation of Seismic Hazards in URM (Unreinforced Masonry) Buildings', *National Science Foundation Topical Report 08*, ABK, A Joint Venture, Jan., pp. 2-4.

McKee, H. (1980) *Masonry*, National Trust/Columbia University Series, Washington DC.

Ruskin, J. (1901) n ?? *The Seven Lamps of Architecture*.London: George Allen.

Seamon, D. & Mugerauer, R. (1985) *Dwelling, Place and Environment: Towards a Phenomenology of Person and World*, Martin Nijhoff, Dordrecht.

Shapiro, Daniel (1998) 'National guidelines and commentary for the seismic rehabilitation of buildings', in *Disaster Management Programs for Historic Sites*, eds Dirk H. R. Spennemann & David W. Look. San Francisco and Albury: Association for Preservation Technology (Western Chapter) and The Johnstone Centre, Charles Sturt University. Pp. 91-92.

15
National guidelines and commentary for the seismic rehabilitation of buildings

DANIEL SHAPIRO [¶]

The ultimate in seismic mitigation is damage reduction through rehabilitation. In the Standards of Seismic Safety for Existing Federally Owned or Leased Buildings historic buildings are not treated differently on the premise that earthquakes do not differentiate between the general building stock and historic buildings and hence seismic rehabilitation procedures must be universally applicable.

However, there are aspects of seismic rehabilitation of historic buildings that may be unique and the Guidelines will direct design professionals' attention to these aspects.

The Guidelines will be one of the first documents to introduce performance-based design. This will provide flexibility not available in current codes and standards to tailor designs to specific performance objectives.

Performance-based design, including descriptions of damage states corresponding to the performance levels, is described in the Guidelines. Levels are:

- Collapse prevention

- Life safety

- Immediate occupancy

[¶] Shapiro Okino Hom & Associates, Structural Engineers, 303 2nd Street, Suite 305 South, San Francisco, California, CA 94107, USA

A Basic Safety Objective has been established for the Guidelines. It is defined as meeting the life safety performance level for the standard design earthquake (presently defined as an earthquake with a 10% change of exceedence in 500 years) and meeting the collapse prevention performance level for the maximum expected earthquake (presently defined as an earthquake with a 10% chance of exceedence in 2,500 years). However, a designer may select other design objectives which may be either enhanced or limited, offering the designer a spectrum of choices to suit his or her requirements.

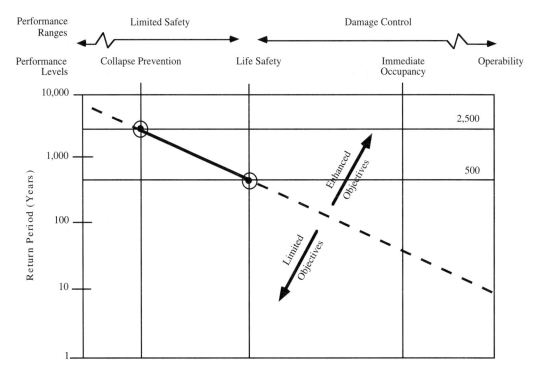

Figure 15.1 Basic safety performance objectives

16

The Secretary of the Interior's Standards for Rehabilitation pertinent to cultural resources affected by disasters

STEPHEN A. MATHISON [¶]

The State of Washington has not recently had a major disaster that has affected many historic or cultural resources. The eruption of Mount St. Helens in 1980 certainly affected some known and many unknown archaeological sites, but had little impact on historic resources. Floods and windstorms have some effects, but not to a major degree. Recently a mild earthquake south of Seattle damaged a Carnegie library in a small community.

However, we are told that a major earthquake could occur at any time and that its impact could be felt throughout western Washington. It is, of course, fortunate that we have not experienced many major disasters, but it also presents a problem because there is a sense of complacency, particularly when it comes to planning and mitigating for disasters. Response and recovery training is given far more attention than planning or funding for pre-event stabilization measures.

When speaking about the Secretary of the Interior's Standards for Rehabilitation, I usually focus on Standard No. 6 as their essence. It basically says that deteriorated historic features shall be repaired rather than replaced, that severely deteriorated features should be replaced 'in kind', and missing elements should be replicated based on solid documentation.

[¶] Architectural Designer, Office of Archaeology and Historic Preservation, Department of Community Development,
111 21st Avenue, SW, Olympia, WA 98504-8343, USA

Mitigation measures I deal with, in regard to the Standards, are usually pretty straightforward and fundamental - for example:

- Tying floors and roofs to walls and parapets to roofs in unreinforced masonry buildings. The primary battles here are whether or not wall ties must penetrate through walls, and if so, their spacing, configuration and finish.

- The introduction of shear walls that will not only accomplish adequate stabilization of structures, but also do as little damage or removal of significant historic features as possible.

- The seismic bracing of buildings, particularly those with 'soft-stories'. This is one of the most difficult measures to achieve because structural engineers and building officials will often tell us that adequate and cost effective stabilization cannot be done without cross-bracing which would be visible through existing windows. Often, after periods of negotiation, such elements can be redesigned, but sometimes a certain number of these intrusive elements must be accepted. Some have been approved for Investment Tax Credits by the National Park Service, if the bracing is painted out a neutral color.

Other common problem areas are retention of room and corridor configurations, replacement of doors and closing of transoms for fire safety, and window replacement.

For most projects involving the Standards, whether they be hazard mitigation related or not, negotiation between all parties involved is very important, including local preservation and building officials, architects, engineers, building owners and sometimes funding agents. While our State Historic Building Code is not mandatory unless adopted by local jurisdictions, it is often used as a guideline for designated properties by designers and local building officials in conjunction with Section 104(f) of the Uniform Building Code or the Uniform Code for Building Conservation.

Craigo, Steade (1998) 'Case study: earthquakes', in *Disaster Management Programs for Historic Sites*, eds Dirk H. R. Spennemann & David W. Look. San Francisco and Albury: Association for Preservation Technology (Western Chapter) and The Johnstone Centre, Charles Sturt University. Pp. 95-98.

17
Case study: earthquakes

STEADE CRAIGO [¶]

The January 1994 Northridge Earthquake struck hard: the first major earthquake to occur directly beneath a highly urbanized area in California. Northridge was the first California earthquake and first disaster to receive a special grant totaling US$10 million to preserve damaged historic properties. This grant program is administered by the Historic Preservation Partners for Earthquake Response, a coalition of national, state and local preservation agencies.

Several significant changes were made by the preservationist community to respond to the Northridge disaster and to mitigate the threat to historic sites. These were developed as a result of the difficult learning process provided by the earlier disasters, such as the Loma Prieta Earthquake.

Earthquakes are the most insidious of all *natural* disasters, putting aside man-made disasters. There is not an earthquake season such as for hurricanes. Earthquakes do not appear on weather radar. They strike without warning, and have almost everywhere in the continental United States, and elsewhere in the world, such as recently in Japan and in Russia; and there is never just one quake. After the Loma Prieta Earthquake, over 1,000 aftershocks were felt, some almost as strong as the first.

When the buildings begin to shake, bridges sway and the sidewalks and roads move, the first thought is "Is this only a minor tremor, or is it the BIG ONE!"

Earthquakes are both physically and emotionally devastating to the population. They can wreck the physical infrastructure - the gas, electrical and communications lines which we are so depended upon. The local, regional and state economies can be decimated. Thousands of people can be left homeless or in makeshift shelters.

[¶] Historical Architect California Office of Historic Preservation, California Department of Parks and Recreation, PO Box 942896, Sacramento, CA 94296-0001, USA. E-mail: calshpo@quiknet.com

The basic nature of earthquake disasters has historically remained the same to this day. The photographs and written records of the 1886 Charleston, South Carolina Earthquake and the 1906 San Francisco Earthquake and Fire document this point.

The 1989 Loma Prieta Earthquake was truly a 'wake-up call' for preservationists. We saw how vulnerable historic sites are in a disaster. All the protective regulations and processes that we have struggled to implement in the last two decades do not exist during that emergency period following the initial earthquake disaster.

The California Environmental Quality Act, which covers both natural and cultural resources, Section 106 of the National Historic Preservation Act, and local protective laws and property rights are superseded by emergency needs. Historic buildings damaged in the Loma Prieta Earthquake were demolished in the name of 'life safety'.

Local government officials, especially the smaller towns and cities, were overwhelmed by the impacts of the disaster. Responding to the basic needs of shelter, water, food, communications, power, and restoring the local economies were the high priorities. Preserving or giving historic building a second opinion before demolition was not a high priority.

Figure 17.1. Commercial building in Hollywood, CA, partially collapsed following the 1994 Northridge Earthquake. It was restored using special federal funds for damaged historic structures. (Photo: Steade Craigo 1994).

Further, disaster response information was very confused among the local government officials, and the federal and state disaster agencies. This situation led to the demolition of many historic buildings, especially the unreinforced masonry structures which were very quickly demolished in the first 30 days of the disaster.

Also, funding for repairs was extremely limited. Federal and state agencies provided almost 100% funding for government and nonprofit owned buildings. But for damaged private buildings, such as residential and commercial buildings, and also religious buildings there was basically nothing except low-interest loans.

Figure 17.2. A private residence in Fillmore, CA, following the 1994 Northridge Earthquake. (Photo: Steade Craigo 1994).

We quickly understood that the state preservation agencies had no official disaster role. Our own fellow state agency, the Office of Emergency Services did not recognize the Office of Historic Preservation and the California State Historic Building Safety Board as partnerships in the disaster response.

Another interesting discovery was that the local governments with strong preservation programs already in place lost the least smallest number of historic structures and also recovered very quickly, such as San Francisco and the City of Los Gatos. Unfortunately, other cities, such as Watsonville and Santa Cruz, lost many historic buildings and their recovery has been very slow.

The rush of demolitions was slowed somewhat by a new state law, Public Resources Code 5028, which requires the approval of the State Office of Historic Preservation before a historic building can be demolished, if an imminent threat situation does not exist.

Several years after the Loma Prieta Earthquake, a formal agreement was reached between the State Office of Historic Preservation and the Office of Emergency Services, which provided the Office of Historic Preservation with an official disaster role.

Figure 17.3. A private residence in Santa Cruz, CA., following the 1994 Northridge Earthquake. Wood frame residential structures were commonly damaged when the foundation cripple walls collapsed. (Photo: Steade Craigo 1994).

The Loma Prieta and the Humboldt Earthquakes clearly demonstrated the need to educate the public and government agencies, and to seismically retrofit buildings, as well as to be prepared. We could no longer bury our heads in the concrete, ignoring the next earthquake.

Winter, Thomas A. (1998) 'Impact of the Northridge
Earthquake on the Garnier Building, Los Encinos State
Historic Park', in *Disaster Management Programs for
Historic Sites*, eds Dirk H. R. Spennemann & David W.
Look. San Francisco and Albury: Association for
Preservation Technology (Western Chapter) and The
Johnstone Centre, Charles Sturt University. Pp. 99-110.

18

Impact of the Northridge Earthquake on the Garnier Building, Los Encinos State Historic Park

THOMAS A. WINTER [¶]

The subject project is an 1872 two-story stone structure in the San Fernando Valley of Los Angeles, California. The site is on Ventura Boulevard (old Highway 101): west of the 405 Freeway and about 5 miles (8 km) from the Northridge Earthquake epicenter. The property consists of a small site with a core of historic structures that constitute the prime resources of a historic park.

The Garnier Building in Los Encinos State Historic Park is a two-story building of rough limestone random ashlar and lime mortar construction. The walls are approximately 18 inches (45.7 cm) thick and are plastered on each side with a lime plaster approximately 1 inch (2.54 cm) thick. The building is 26.5 feet (7.95 m) by 45 feet (13.5 m) and approximately 23 feet (6.9 m) tall to the eaves walls; the gable end walls are over 30 feet (9 m) tall at the peak. There is a partial basement on the northern half of the building with a 6.5 feet (1.95 m) height to joists.

The structure was retrofitted with an earthquake bracing and tying scheme in 1989. This scheme installed 17 inch by 0.75 inch (43.2 cm) and diameter 1.9 cm steel anchors in epoxy grouted holes at 2 feet (61 cm) on center around the perimeter of both floors and the ceiling. A shear wall with footing was installed in a location approximately on the line of a historic wall between the first and second floor - which was approximately at the third point from the southern end of the structure. Diaphragms and chords were

[¶] Associate Architect, Northern Service Center, California Department of Parks and Recreation, 1725 23rd Street, Suite 200, Sacramento, California, CA 95816, USA. E-mail: Tom_Winter@bbs.macnexus.org

developed on each floor and the ceiling line. The high gable end walls were braces to the ceiling diaphragm.

The earthquake damaged the northern end (short) wall which was farthest from the shear wall. Severe cracking caused the corners to separate from the rest of the masonry and holes to develop at the panels between the windows on the first floor. The west side (long) wall was cracked at each panel between the windows. After the earthquake, immediate stabilization was done by installing a temporary shear and support wall near the damaged north wall. The masonry, restrained at the floor lines, remains in plane along with the majority of the wall surfaces which are intact.

Repair assumptions

There were several initial assumptions which are a part of the California State Park approach to dealing with a damaged historic structure:

- The buildings must be restored or 'fixed' with as little alteration as possible.

- The original fabric will be saved to the degree possible. This is tempered with the 'cost reality' that the higher the costs the less likely the repairs will be accomplished within a timely period and, in the case of re-occurring events such as earthquakes, the future reliability of the 'fix' in such events must be considered.

- There are archaeological resources in and around the structures that must be protected, avoided or mitigated.

The process

Since this was a federally declared disaster, a process was established to receive federal disaster aid funds to repair the damage. From the State Park's point of view the damage has closed a small park with a small total attendance and limited funds for repairs are not allocated to the park on an 'emergency' basis. Funds for the state match will need to be budgeted through the normal process, which involves putting them into the district maintenance budget to compete with other maintenance projects. Currently, only a small percentage of projects are funded from the lists of potential park maintenance projects.

The budgets for the maintenance projects are made up each Spring. The Federal Emergency Management Agency (FEMA) has provided US$4,500 for preliminary Architecture and Engineering which could be spent immediately, but the 10% match must be identified to the budget office before the funds can be encumbered. The FEMA money is reimbursable and state money must be spent first, then reimbursed. The California State Park Director has authorized spending the money, as long as the match is identified.

Staff time will be used as match, but the majority of the work is engineering in nature and the department has no structural engineers. That means that the engineering must be contracted so no match can be achieved towards construction.

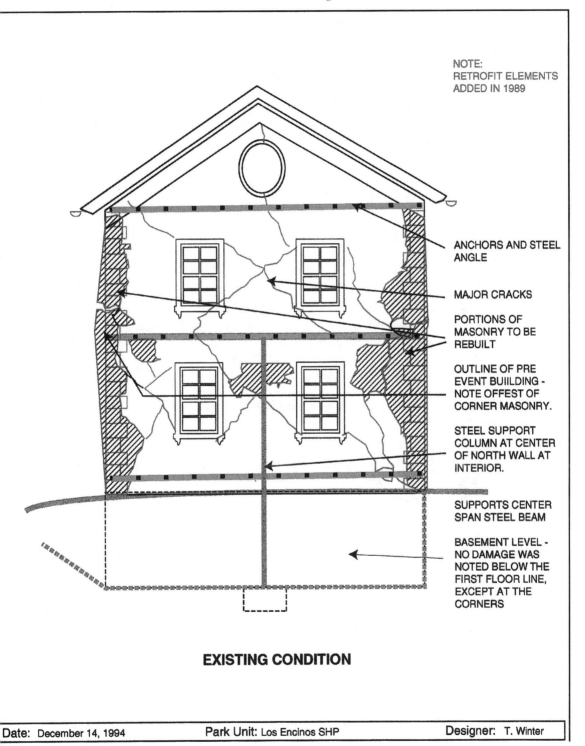

NOTE:
RETROFIT ELEMENTS
ADDED IN 1989

ANCHORS AND STEEL
ANGLE

MAJOR CRACKS

PORTIONS OF
MASONRY TO BE
REBUILT

OUTLINE OF PRE
EVENT BUIILDING -
NOTE OFFEST OF
CORNER MASONRY.

STEEL SUPPORT
COLUMN AT CENTER
OF NORTH WALL AT
INTERIOR.

SUPPORTS CENTER
SPAN STEEL BEAM

BASEMENT LEVEL -
NO DAMAGE WAS
NOTED BELOW THE
FIRST FLOOR LINE,
EXCEPT AT THE
CORNERS

EXISTING CONDITION

Date: December 14, 1994   Park Unit: Los Encinos SHP   Designer: T. Winter

Figure 18.1 Garnier Building: north elevation. Existing condition following Loma Prieta, Dec. 1994. (Drawing: Thomas Winter 1994).

There were a total of five buildings damaged at this site by the 'quake. An overall estimate of the cost of repair is in the area of US$1 million dollars. The match is US$100,000 and that amount is a large portion of the district maintenance budget for one year. Because of the match requirement each step of the project, Preliminary Architect and Engineering, Architect and Engineering and Construction are taking a long time to realize - although without FEMA reimbursement these buildings might never be repaired.

Existing conditions

The retrofit performed as expected during the Northridge event. The walls were tied to the horizontal diaphragms and remain in plane at those locations. The retrofit did not keep the building from suffering significant damage, but life safety was maintained.

Damage to the structure was worst on the narrow, tall gable end walls, and the west side wall which has a row of six openings in each floor level creating a 'frame' structure situation. The east elevation, with fewer openings, was considerably stronger and acted as a diaphragm with punched openings.

The north elevation suffered severe cracking such that the area between the lower windows collapsed, leaving two small piers of masonry supporting the continuous header over the windows. The building corners, which had no anchors within the width of the wall, dislodged and are immanently in danger of collapse. The lack of corner anchors has been noted as a deficiency and current unreinforced masonry design includes corner anchors. The masonry above the second-floor windows remains in good condition with little cracking. This masonry was tied into the roof and second-floor ceiling structure during the retrofit.

The west elevation exhibits 'X' cracks at each 'pier' below the windows. There appears to be little, if any, amount of out-of-plane offset in the cracks, since this area is tied to the floor by anchors. The lower floor 'piers' area also cracked.

The south wall exhibits fewer diagonal cracks since it is protected by a shear wall located one third of the building length from the south wall. The cracks range from hairline to 0.5 inch (1.27 cm).

The doors and windows along three sides of the structure are operable, indicating little, if any, post-event racking of the masonry. The lower windows on the north elevation were damaged by the initial flexing or subsequent collapse of the masonry holding them.

Repairs and retrofit

Damage to the structure can be divided into three areas, based on the severity of the damage. Area one - the north wall; area two - the west wall; area three - the south and east walls.

BOTH CORNERS
HAVE DISLODGED

MASONRY FALLEN
OUT UNDER
HEADER

Date: December 16, 1994   Park Unit: Los Encinos SHP   Designer: T. Winter

Figure 18.2 Garnier Building: north elevation. Existing condition following Loma Prieta, Dec. 1994. (Photo: Thomas Winter 1994).

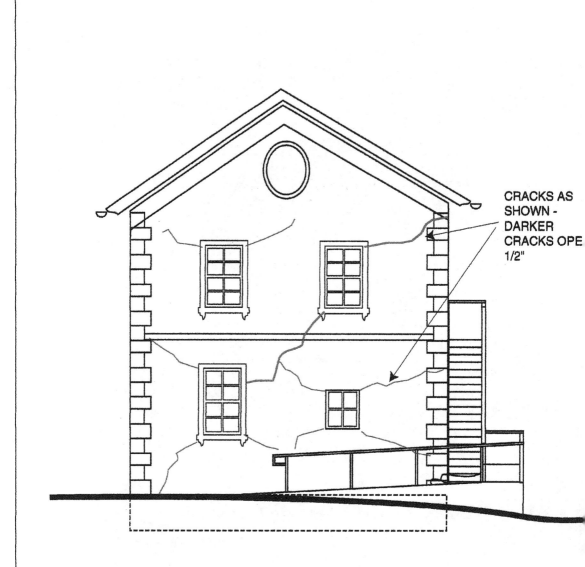

CRACKS AS
SHOWN -
DARKER
CRACKS OPE
1/2"

SOUTH ELEVATION
EXISTING CONDITIONS

Date: December, 1994   Park Unit: Los Encinos SHP   Designer: T. Winter

Figure 18.3 Garnier Building: south elevation. Existing condition following Loma Prieta, Dec. 1994. (Photo: Thomas Winter 1994).

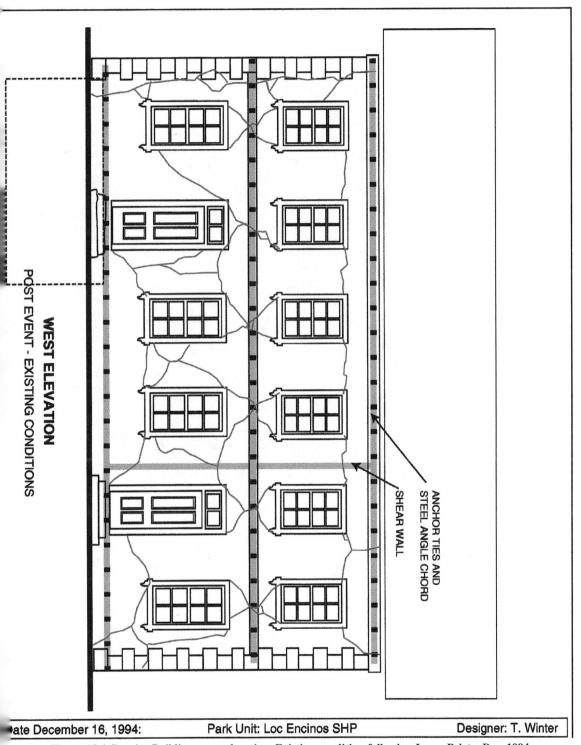

WEST ELEVATION

POST EVENT - EXISTING CONDITIONS

SHEAR WALL

ANCHOR TIES AND
STEEL ANGLE CHORD

Date December 16, 1994:   Park Unit: Loc Encinos SHP   Designer: T. Winter

**Figure 18.4 Garnier Building: west elevation. Existing condition following Loma Prieta, Dec. 1994.
(Photo: Thomas Winter 1994).**

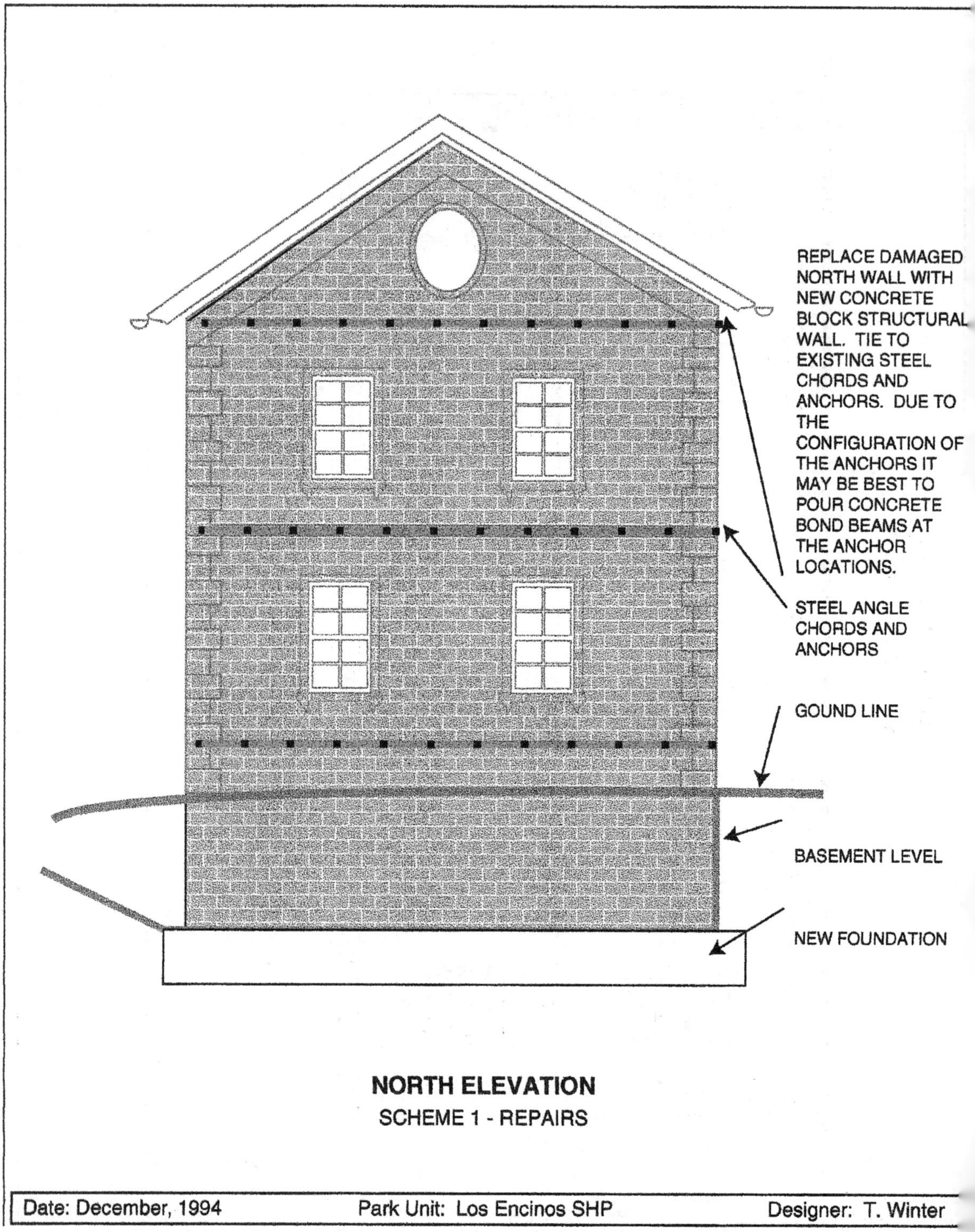

REPLACE DAMAGED NORTH WALL WITH NEW CONCRETE BLOCK STRUCTURAL WALL. TIE TO EXISTING STEEL CHORDS AND ANCHORS. DUE TO THE CONFIGURATION OF THE ANCHORS IT MAY BE BEST TO POUR CONCRETE BOND BEAMS AT THE ANCHOR LOCATIONS.

STEEL ANGLE CHORDS AND ANCHORS

GOUND LINE

BASEMENT LEVEL

NEW FOUNDATION

NORTH ELEVATION
SCHEME 1 - REPAIRS

| Date: December, 1994 | Park Unit: Los Encinos SHP | Designer: T. Winter |

Figure 18.5 Garnier Building: north elevation. Mitigation Scheme One. (Drawing: Thomas Winter 1994).

During the retrofit process, nearly two hundred 1-inch (2.54 cm) holes were cored into the masonry to within 1 inch (2.54 cm) of the outside to insert the tie rods. The first holes were then 'filled' with epoxy before inserting the 0.75-inch (1.9 cm) anchor rods. Considerable epoxy was needed to fill the holes and it was determined that the wall contained a large amount of void space. The anchors were subsequently fitted with screens which lessened the amount of epoxy required.

The void space can now be used to strengthen the wall. Filling the voids with a relatively strong grout is possible since the limestone is quite hard. The new cracks can be filled with a similar grout. A grouting consultant is required to do a test panel on the building to determine the extent to which the wall will take grout, the spacing of the grout ports, and accurate cost data.

It is anticipated that all of the existing rock masonry will be treated as described above.

Area One: North wall
Three schemes have been analyzed for the most badly damaged wall. The three schemes have differing amounts of intervention but each attempts to arrive at a similar seismic resistance.

Scheme One
This removes all of the wall and replaces it with a new concrete block wall. This solution is simple but requires demolition of all of the original historic fabric of the wall. The thickness of the original masonry is about 18 inches (45.7 cm), the widest block is 12 inches (30.5 cm); either the wall must be furred to the proper thickness or the block could be set sideways to make a 16-inch (40.6-cm) wall and plastered to the appropriate thickness. The furring could be constructed of original masonry, but since there is no indication of the masonry underlying the plaster it is not cost effective. There are several variations of how the wall could be configured in the basement level, but scheme one costs are based on removing the existing masonry, excavating and installing a footing.

The masonry will be tied to the structure through the existing steel angle and new grout anchors, which can be cast into the block or into a bond beam poured at that level. The block/bond beam must be set flush with the black of the angle to assure shear transfer.

Due to the cost of demolition, excavation and reconstruction, this scheme is the most costly. It is also the most damaging to the historic fabric.

Scheme Two
This removes the most badly damaged portion of the wall and replaces it with a block, shotcrete or poured concrete shear wall. The damaged and offset corners can be demolished and rebuilt with matching masonry, or be formed and shot or poured back with a concrete mix. The remaining portion of the wall would need to be pressure grouted after the cracks, holes and other damage have been repaired. New anchors will be placed in the corners tied to the steel angles.

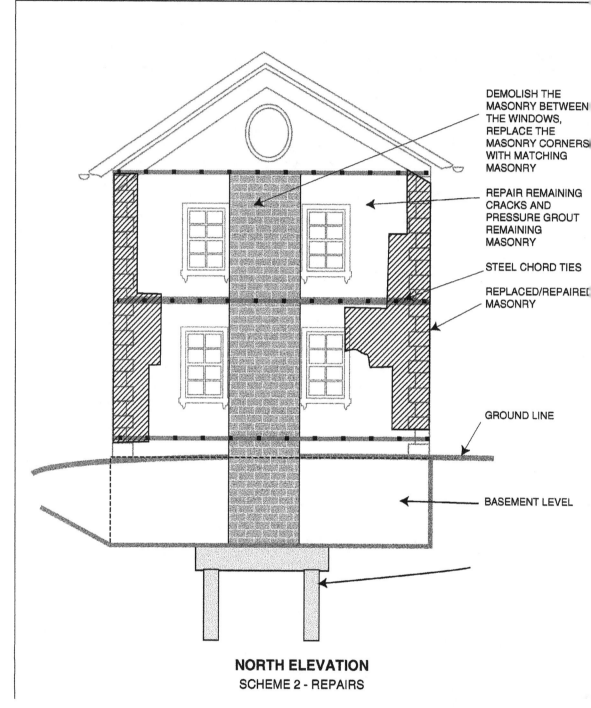

DEMOLISH THE
MASONRY BETWEEN
THE WINDOWS,
REPLACE THE
MASONRY CORNERS
WITH MATCHING
MASONRY

REPAIR REMAINING
CRACKS AND
PRESSURE GROUT
REMAINING
MASONRY

STEEL CHORD TIES

REPLACED/REPAIRED
MASONRY

GROUND LINE

BASEMENT LEVEL

NORTH ELEVATION
SCHEME 2 - REPAIRS

Figure 18.6 Garnier Building: north elevation. Mitigation Scheme Two. (Drawing: Thomas Winter 1994).

The shear wall must be constructed through the basement, and will require a footing and probably piles or piers to develop the lateral resistance required.

This scheme is the least costly and appears to be a viable alternative. Damage to the historic fabric is relatively minor and is perhaps the least. The ties between the angle chord and the new shear wall become very important and must be calculated to assure their adequacy.

This scheme requires that the site be excavated. The cost of archaeological monitoring and testing is not added into the cost estimate, but would be considerable.

Scheme Three
This requires the least demolition; only the displace corners would need to be removed and reconstructed. The holes will be built up of matching masonry. The foundation appears to have suffered little damage and can be reused.

To carry the seismic loads better, this wall will be upgraded. The plaster finishes will be removed from the top steel angle chord to the base of the wall and replaced with a reinforced 'structural plaster' which will be tied into the steel angle chords at each level. This scheme assumes that both inside and exterior faces will be treated and tied to each other by steel rods drilled at regular intervals. The plaster will be carried around the corners to tie into the anchors along the long walls. In addition, new corner anchors may be required to secure the corners which failed in this last event.

This scheme retains the most historic masonry but requires that significant amounts of plaster be removed to develop the required strength. The cost is very close to Scheme Two and is therefore a viable alternative.

Since this alternative requires no excavation, a problem in archaeological sensitive sites, it is the preferred alternative. The cost of archaeological monitoring and testing would make Scheme Two more costly.

Area Two: West wall
Only one scheme is proposed for this wall. The general treatment will be to pressure grout the wall and cracks. Some additional strength is required at the points which cracked severely. Structural plaster is proposed for the inside finish where shown on the drawing. This will be tied to the steel chords and into the rock with epoxy anchors at regular intervals.

Area Three: South and east walls
The general treatment should be sufficient to both repair and upgrade these walls to better lateral resistance. That will include pressure grouting the wall and the cracks.

Finishes, furnishings and exhibits

The building was recently rehabilitated as a visitors center. Repair/replacement of damaged finishes, doors and windows is the extent of the work required to bring the building back to its pre-event status. Some damage was done to the exhibits and furnishings, which need to be refinished or replaced as indicated.

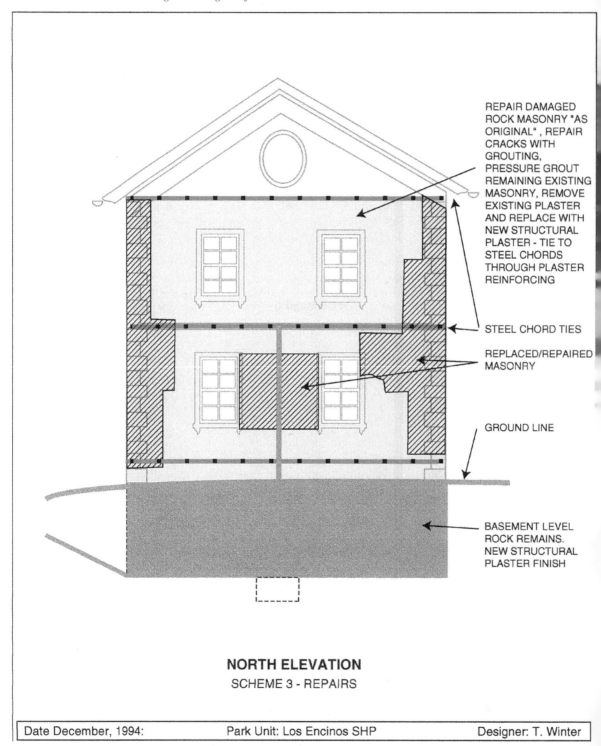

REPAIR DAMAGED ROCK MASONRY "AS ORIGINAL", REPAIR CRACKS WITH GROUTING, PRESSURE GROUT REMAINING EXISTING MASONRY, REMOVE EXISTING PLASTER AND REPLACE WITH NEW STRUCTURAL PLASTER - TIE TO STEEL CHORDS THROUGH PLASTER REINFORCING

STEEL CHORD TIES

REPLACED/REPAIRED MASONRY

GROUND LINE

BASEMENT LEVEL ROCK REMAINS. NEW STRUCTURAL PLASTER FINISH

NORTH ELEVATION

SCHEME 3 - REPAIRS

Date December, 1994:	Park Unit: Los Encinos SHP	Designer: T. Winter

Figure 18.7 Garnier Building: north elevation. Mitigation Scheme Three. (Drawing: Thomas Winter 1994).

FLOODS AND CYCLONES

19

Conservation management and mitigation of the impact of tropical cyclones on archaeological sites

DIRK H. R. SPENNEMANN ¶

In the following paper, the impact of tropical cyclones on archaeological sites and the effectiveness of the mitigation measures which have been espoused in these cases is assessed. The paper draws on three different examples which vary in terms of geographical spread (Tonga, the Marshall Islands and North Queensland, Australia (Figure 19.1), types of sites (middens, cemeteries, burial monuments) and the level of cultural resource management actions and legislation in place.

Sites on sand dunes

Sites on coastal (and inland) sand dunes are prone to similar erosion processes as open camp sites. Unlike the latter, however, coastal dune systems consist largely of an unconsolidated soil matrix which makes them eminently erodible by wind and wave action. *Dinner-time camps* are discrete dumps of food remains, commonly shellfish, thought to represent a single meal and dumping event by individuals or a small group of people. Ethno-archaeological studies have shown that dinnertime camps were sometimes revisited and a new, discrete dumping event occurred. The archaeologically recognizable food remains varied in amount and species composition. If occupation occurred in well circumscribed areas for a prolonged period of time, or repeatedly over time, the material

---

¶ The Johnstone Centre, Charles Sturt University, PO Box 789, Albury NSW 2640, Australia.
E-mail: dspennemann@csu.edu.au

would accumulate and build up raised heaps of refuse intermingled with soil matrix. These *middens* (shell middens, kitchen middens) are especially conspicuous in coastal areas, where much of the refuse comprises shells which decay much slower than bones or even plant remains (Meehan 1982, pp. 112-115).

Erosion by aeolian action

In the 'normal' course of events, if the vegetation of coastal dunes, especially fore dunes, is disturbed due to impact by (hard-hoofed) animals or people, and partial denudation has occurred, that part of the dune becomes prone to wind erosion. As these disturbances are usually perpendicular to the alignment of the dune, and in line with the main wind direction (ocean to inland), the fine sand particles are blown off towards the inland areas and a 'blowout' is created. As the erosion continues unchecked, the blowout deepens and, with the collapse of the sidewalls, also widens. In addition, the blow-out now provides a convenient way to traverse the dune system and attracts even more animals, people and vehicles using it as a thoroughfare, thus exacerbating the problem (Zallar *et al.* 1979). As a result of this erosion, archaeological sites contained in the dunes, such as middens and burials, are exposed.

Continual wind erosion will remove the matrix of the site and effectively collapse and compact the vertical stratigraphy, leading to a concentration and intermingling of artifacts (of different stratigraphic layers). On a slope, a separation of artifactual material will occur, with rounded artifacts rolling down the slope and thin and lightweight artifacts being blown off by the wind. Lightweight organic matter, such as charcoal and small bones, is also dispersed, with larger bones and shells becoming exposed to photo-degradation and trampling by people and animals. Continued unchecked erosion can combine the artifactual content of midden layers, which originally had been separated by sterile horizons, thus permanently confusing site stratigraphy and chronology.

The impact of the erosion is concentrated and occurs horizontally, increasingly exposing lower deposits. Over time, the erosion will remain localized but widen out. The impact on the archaeological record will also remain localized. If the parameters determining the location of sites are defined by local access points or movement corridors, then it is quite likely that modern livestock/people movement is in a similar, if not identical, location and that significant sites are predominantly affected by the erosion.

Erosion by wave action

If, however, coastal middens are exposed to water and especially wave action, the site will be eroded. The erosion impact is diffuse, affecting a large area of dunes and beach, and it is vertical; that is, one section of the dune is eroded away at a time, with the erosion progressively affecting landward sites. In addition, the artifactual material will be sorted according to size and weight. This is a common phenomenon on any given beach and occurs in shells (Baan 1977, 1978a, 1978b; Lever *et al.* 1964) and sand/gravel sediments (Bird 1984: pp. 143 ff).

Beaches normally undergo a cycle of aggradation and erosions, with 'stable' beachlines in the long-term perspective (Bird 1984). If the sediment cycle is modified by the development of structures interfering with the currents and associated sand movements, or if the beach is subject to recurrent storm surges, then net sediment loss may occur, which has the potential to foreshorten the beach and thus, ultimately, result in the erosion of foredunes and the sites contained therein/thereon.

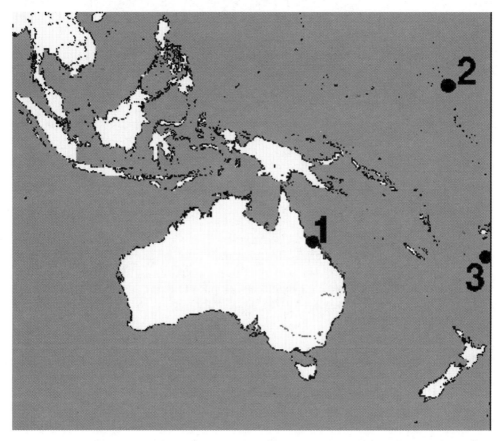

Figure 19.1. Map of the south-west Pacific, showing the location of the sites under discussion. 1-Upstart Bay, North Queensland; 2- Majuro Atoll, Marshall Islands.; 3- Tongatapu, Tonga.

Erosion by storm surge action

The effects of cyclones on the coastal geomorphology of small sand cays and islands have been studied *inter alia* for Tonga (Woodroffe 1983), Jaluit (Blumenstock 1961), Funafuti (Maragos *et al.* 1973) and similar areas. Similar studies for continental shelf areas have been conducted for North Queensland (Hopley 1974a, 1974b). Studies dealing with the impact of cyclones on archaeological sites are few. Bird (1992) has described the impact of cyclones on middens in Queensland, while Hughes and Sullivan (1974) have assessed the impact of storm surges on middens in New South Wales. Spennemann has described the impact of cyclones on sites in Tonga (Spennemann 1987) and the Marshall Islands (Spennemann 1992a). Storm surges and tsunamis have destroyed entire archaeological assemblages on the Siassi Islands of Papua New Guinea (Lilley 1986) and elsewhere in Melanesia, and have been reworking coastal shell-middens in Australia (Hughes & Sullivan 1974) and in the Andaman Islands (Cooper 1985).

Beyond the Pacific, studies have been conducted in the US Virgin Islands and Texas following Hurricane Hugo in 1989 (Gjeesing & Tyson 1990; Nelson 1991). Three of these case studies will be reviewed below:

- Cyclone Isaac on Tongatapu in 1983;

- A high tide at Majuro, Republic of the Marshall Islands in 1980; and

- Cyclones in Queensland, 1988/89.

Cyclone 'Isaac', Tongatapu (1983)

The setting

Tongatapu (21°8' S, 175°12' W) is the southern-most major island of the Tonga group, a raised coral limestone island covered with tephra-derived soils. The island is dominated by a large shallow lagoon in the northern part with extensive mudflats in the northeast. Beginning at the lagoonal mouth, a fringing reef extends to the north-east, which carries a number of small sand cays (Stoddart 1975; Woodroffe 1983). Two of these, Manima and Makaha'a, are of concern here.

Manima is a small oval sand cay, close to the mouth of the inner lagoon, extending some 150 m north-south. The island is covered with coastal broadleaf vegetation and coconut palms (Stoddart 1975; Woodroffe 1983; Spennemann 1986). The eastern and south-eastern shore of the island is dominated by expanses of a sandy beach. Conspicuous are large areas of coarse sediment, which upon close inspection, proves to be the remains of an extensive pottery-bearing midden (TO-Ci-1). Present were shells (mainly *Anadara* sp.), undecorated pottery and volcanic (oven) stones, which do not occur naturally on Tongatapu and must have been imported from volcanic islands in the central part of the Tonga Island chain.

Makaha'a is a small oval sand cay, 310 m long and 170 m in greatest width, on the eastern side of a reef patch isolated from the Tongatapu fringing reefs by a narrow channel about 10 m deep. It is approached through a gap in the encircling reef at its northeast point. The island has aggrading sand beaches on its west and northwest sides and flat (*umu-/*oven) stone spreads fronting eroded sand cliffs on its eastern side. These cliffs are 1.5-2 m high along most of the eastern shore, rising to 3 m in the southeast. Beachrock is extensively exposed, especially in the southeast, and the island is clearly migrating towards the northwest. The eastern cliff is cut in sand, exposing coconut tree roots, and is marked by fallen coconut palms and some large fallen *Hernandia*.

Figure 19.2. An eroded pottery bearing midden in the intertidal zone of Manima Island, Tongatapu, Tonga. The broad dark band indicates the spread of stone material, pottery and large shells. The narrow dark band at the left of the image indicates the high tide mark demarcated by seaweed. (Photo: Dirk Spennemann 1986).

Impact of the cyclone

Tropical Cyclone Isaac, which hit Tonga on 3 March 1982, was undoubtedly one of the worst storms which Tonga has experienced this century. It claimed six lives and caused enormous devastation to buildings and crops. The cyclone developed about 160 km northeast of Western Samoa and traveled southwest at an average speed of 12 knots, traveling directly over the Ha'apai Group and passing some 50 km northwest of Tongatapu.

In Nuku'alofa, a peak gust of 92 knots was measured. Cyclone Isaac coincided with a high spring tide of 1.2 m at Nuku'alofa. Since no tide gauge was in operation at the time of the storm, no exact record of the height of the storm surge is available. Extensive flooding of coastal areas on the northern coast and the fact that Nuku'alofa was entirely under water, testify that the water was several meters above the high-tide level. Much of the storm surge associated with Cyclone Isaac must have been buffered by the great width of reef flat along this coast (Oliver & Reardon 1982; Woodroffe 1983; Spennemann 1987).

On the islet of *Manima*, a pottery-bearing shell midden was completely eroded, today only recognizable as a band of shell and stones in the intertidal zone (Figure 19.2). A close-up view shows that only the heavy elements remain, such as oven stones, large shells and pottery (Figure 19.3), the fine material having been washed out.

Figure 19.3. Close-up of a pottery-bearing midden site in the intertidal zone of Manima Island, Tongatapu, Tonga. The dark spots in the photographs are volcanic oven stones, the rest are shells and some potsherds. Charcoal and fine sediment has been washed out. (Photo: Dirk Spennemann 1986).

The first archaeological survey to take place on *Makaha'a* was conducted in 1957 by Jack Golson. He noted a stone-lined (chiefly) burial mound on the east side of the island; it was badly eroding, with more than half of the site already washed into the sea. He also noted a burial vault, just visible in the profile. His excavation proved that the mound consisted of two construction phases, an earlier house or settlement mound and a later use as a burial mound. On the occasion of the 1986 survey of Makaha'a, no trace of the stone lining could be seen and the burial vault mentioned by Golson was standing in the middle of the beach, some 2 to 3 m in front of the present sand cliff (Spennemann 1987). Only a small part (approximately 1 m) of the earth mound is still visible. Since 1957, at least 5 m of shoreline has been eroded here (Figure 19.4).

Cultural resource management actions

In the absence of a Tongan National Heritage Management Authority at the time, the cultural resource management action taken consisted of a survey in 1986, which was conducted as part of the author's survey for his Ph.D. fieldwork. Erosion was also noted on other islands and recorded (for example, Spennemann 1986, 1987). In all cases, artifactual material was collected, as was the case on other sites on the main island. A report of the extent of the erosion and damage to the sites was drawn up for the Ministry of Lands, Survey and Natural Resources, which dealt with matters concerning land management (Spennemann 1986). No further action was taken.

Figure 19.4. A burial chamber of a chiefly burial mound, exposed by storm surge erosion of the coastline. Makaha'a Island, Tongatapu, Tonga. The photos show the appearance of the chamber at low (top) and high tide (bottom) (Photos: Dirk Spennemann 1986).

Figure 19.5. Impact of the 1979 high tide event on a cemetery at Uliga Island, Majuro Atoll (Photo: Carol Curtis 1979).

The exposure and erosion of the burial chamber at Makaha'a allowed, for the first and only time, to look at the make-up of a stone-lined burial vault. A human humerus, found wedged in under a fallen slab, thought to originate from the vault, was dated to 690 ± 180 BP (ANU-5716), thus providing the first direct date for a burial in a vault.

Implications

The storm surges destroyed several sites *in toto* and reduced others to relatively meaningless jumbles of intermingled material derived from (possibly) various phases. The late, undecorated pottery on Tongatapu is not very diagnostic (Spennemann 1989a) and with the removal of datable material (charcoal, shell) such midden sites have lost almost all their potential for analysis. This needs to be seen in the context of the horticultural potential of the sand cays compared to the fertile tephra soils of the main island, with the differences in site location likely to be a reflection of different site function. One of the major problems thus posed is that some site types, of which there are only a few (given the size of the sand cays), are disproportionately more prone to decay by storm surges.

High tide Majuro Atoll (1990)

The setting

Majuro Atoll, situated at 7°03' to 7°13' N   and 171°02' to 171° 23' E, measuring about 45 km (30 miles) by 11 km (7 miles) in dimensions, is oriented ENE to WSW and covers a total lagoon area of 295 sq km with a total land area of only 9.17 sq km. The atoll can be split into a north-western, windward side and a south-eastern, leeward one. The north-western part is characterized by large, extended reef flats with very few islands, save for the distinct Enyagin group, which is located at the very north-western tip of the atoll and which consists of two reasonably large islands: Jelte and Rongrong. Towards the east, the islands on the northern side become more numerous and are relatively closely spaced. Located there are the three most populated islands: Djarrit, Uliga and Delap.

Figure 19.6. A burial monument of the Laura Cemetery, collapsed onto the beach after the 1990 high tides on Majuro Atoll, Republic of the Marshall Islands. (Photo: Dirk Spennemann 1990).

The southern side of the atoll consisted, until 1905, of a single continuous island reaching from Rairok to Laura. The typhoons of 1905 and 1918 disrupted this continuous island, especially in its eastern part. In the south-west, the island is still intact, largely only 200 to 300 m wide, with the largest land mass, Laura (Majuro Island) at its western end (US Army Corps of Engineers 1989; Spennemann 1992b). Laura cemetery, site MI-Mj-20, is located at the lagoon side of Majuro Atoll, some 100 m south of the actual tip of Majuro Island. The site consists of an array of concrete grave enclosures and concrete grave monuments. According to historic evidence, the cemetery was in use in the 1910s and 1920s and contains a number of significant graves.

Impact of the cyclone

Stable high pressure systems north-east of Eneen-Kio (Wake Island) or east of the Marshall Islands can create higher-than-normal sea levels which will cause flooding of low-lying areas if they coincide with a spring tide, or with higher wave action. Such high pressure systems are common and have affected the atolls of the Marshall Islands on numerous occasions (the 1979, 1989, 1990 and 1991 floods on Majuro Atoll for example). During 13 and 14 November 1989, an exceptionally high tide occurred on Majuro Atoll which was connected with heavy swells stemming from a high pressure cell. The high tide caused substantial erosion of parts of the lagoonal shoreline on many parts of the atoll, but especially at the northern tip of Majuro Island where some 3 m in depth disappeared. The wave action had caused several coconut palms to topple over and resulted in substantial erosion of a historic cemetery, which already had been partially eroded in the years before. The eroding shoreline exposed a number of burials and caused other burial vaults to collapse (Figure 19.6). On the visits following the erosion, several bones were found scattered on the beach and a thorough search was made for other bones. All bones were lying in the inter-tidal zone, intermixed with coral rubble and other debris.

Figure 19.7. Burial monuments of the Laura Cemetery, collapsed onto the beach after the 1990 high tides on Majuro Atoll, Republic of the Marshall Islands. (Photo: Dirk Spennemann 1990).

Cultural resource management actions

The management actions espoused by the Historic Preservation Office of the Republic of the Marshall Islands, was to investigate the tip of Laura on the day after the high tide to monitor the extent of erosion. This occurred mainly as part of long-ranging interest in the geomorphological changes on Majuro Atoll; a survey of the effects of the erosion was conducted by the author on repeated occasions. In the process, the erosion of the cemetery was noted and all human bones found on the beach were picked up. This was repeated a couple of days later. The bones were identified (see below) and prepared for reburial, which took some time to be organized. Discussions with relevant local planning authorities (Environment Protection Authority, Capital Infrastructure Program, Majuro Local Government) ensued, resulting in the conclusion that any protection against further erosion was impossible in view of both the costs involved and the potential for increased erosion at other localities due to shoreline protection works at the cemetery. It was then raised to move the cemetery to a new location, further inland, but public and informal calls through the traditional channels brought little response as to whose relatives are buried there. As it was felt that reburial without permission of every descendant involved would not be appropriate, the initiative was called off. Thus, overall, the management was reactive, content to document the changes and the impact.

Implications

Given their location close to the shore, and given the relative instability of the shorelines of the islands making up an atoll, eroding cemeteries are a common occurrence in the Marshall Islands (Spennemann 1990a) and isolated human bones are often found in the inter-tidal zone (Adams *et al.* 1990; Spennemann 1989a , 1990b , 1990c 1990d). More often than not, however, the human remains recovered are isolated pieces, mainly of the cranium or long bones. The differential sorting of beach sediments as discussed above, also applies to human bones of cemeteries eroding due to water and wave action. The underlying phenomenon is the differential in the velocity of the water, and hence its capability to move heavier, and hence larger, items of the same material. In addition, some of the human remains have a natural buoyancy (such as the vertebrae which are filled with spongiotic cavities trapping air) which facilitates sea-borne movement. Table 19.1 shows the representation of human remains found on the shore near the Laura cemetery.

Table 19.1. Representation of human remains found on the beach (Majuro Atoll).

Class	Percentage	Bones involved
I	100-85%	Cranium, Mandible
II	85-50%	Tibia, Femur, Humerus, Fibula
III	50-25%	Pelvis, Radius, Ulna, Axis, Clavicula
IV	25-10%	V. cervicalis, Costae, Atlas, Os sacrum
V	10-0%	Patella, V. lumbalis, V. thoracica, Metacarpus, Phalanges manus, Scapula, Ossa carpalia, Tarsus, Astragalus, Ossa tarsalia, Metatarsus, Phalanges pedis

The two major factors involved in the observed differential preservation of skeletal elements appear to be (i) the overall weight of the bone and (ii) its ability to float. Light-weighted bones, such as the phalanges, or heavily spongiotic bones, such as vertebrae and patellae, float easily and - by wave and tidal action - can be carried out to sea, leaving the heavier bones, such as femora, tibiae, or non-floating bones, such as the crania and mandibles, behind. Given the thorough search for bones along the shoreline, both parallel and perpendicular to the water's edge, the differential representation observed is not a factor of selective recovery. However, the overall size of a bone is, on the whole, correlated with its overall weight which is the determining factor in sediment distribution along beach transects.

It needs to be kept in mind however, that the impact of the high tide system was limited. The impact of devastating typhoons is on record for the Marshall Islands. These have eroded entire islets down to the bare reef platform, washing everything on it (houses, people, trees, soil) into the lagoon or sea (cf., Spennemann & Marschner 1994   for compilation).

Cyclones North Queensland (1988/89)

The setting

Upstart Bay is located about 120 km south of Townsville, Queensland, between Cape Upstart and the southern end of the Burdekin River delta. The sandy beach of a shallow bay measures 13 km in length and comprises a narrow band of Holocene foredunes backed by a series of older beachridges. The beachridges are vegetated with coastal vines and an open woodland unless modified by blowouts. Archaeological surveys in the early 1980s had located a number of sites, mainly shell middens. This was followed by an intensive survey in 1987 which located and mapped 93 sites (Bird 1992).

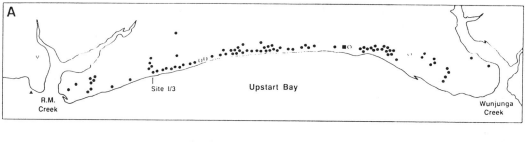

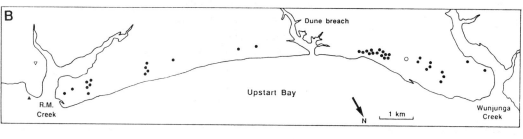

• Shell midden/scatter   ○ Midden complex   ◻ Artefact scatter   ■ Burial   ▲ Fishtrap   ▽ Quartzite quarry

Figure 19.8. Distribution of archaeological sites at Upstart Bay, N. Queensland before (left) and after (right) the cyclones 'Charlie' and 'Aivu' (after Bird 1992).

Impact of the cyclone

Cyclone 'Charlie' made landfall on 1 March 1988. The cyclone reached gusts of 160 km/h and created a maximum storm surge of 0.5 m at the nearest recording station, Bowen. Bird (1992) assumes the local surge height to be greater given the inshore topography of the bay. The typhoon surge breached the dune system and created an estuary at a point where the dune had been degraded by human interference. Of the 93 sites found in 1987, fourteen (15%) were completely destroyed as a result of the cyclone, and a further 23 (25%) were substantially impaired. Some of the sites in the foredune were truncated, while the seaward margins of others were reworked. The sites not affected by wave action seemed to exhibit evidence of deflation by aeolian action (Bird 1992).

Cyclone 'Aivu' made landfall on 4 April 1989. The cyclone reached wind gusts of up to 200 km/h, with a maximum recorded storm surge of 1.2 m. Again, the local storm surge at Upstart Bay was much greater, approximately 3 m on the outgoing high tide. The storm surge caused substantial foredune erosion and recession of beaches; as a collateral a large number of archaeological sites was affected. Of the 78 archaeological sites that survived cyclone 'Charlie', 37 were destroyed and a further five were modified or otherwise impaired (Bird 1992).

The eroding shoreline dramatically reduced the number of sites, especially in the central section of the bay (Figure 19.8). If we compare the loss of sites from 1987 to 1988, then about 40% of all sites were either destroyed are modified as a result of cyclone 'Charlie'. Of the 78 sites surviving from the previous cyclone, another 42 sites were destroyed or (further) modified as result of cyclone 'Aivu'. In the final account, only 39% of all 1987 sites survived the two typhoons unscathed, 6% were reduced or modified and 55% were totally destroyed (Figure 19.9). In the time interval between the two cyclones, no significant redeposition of sediment had occurred and the damaged sites had been exposed to aeolian decay as well. Only in the years after cyclone 'Aivu' did the dune system recover in part - resulting in the reburial of some of the archaeological deposits (Bird 1992).

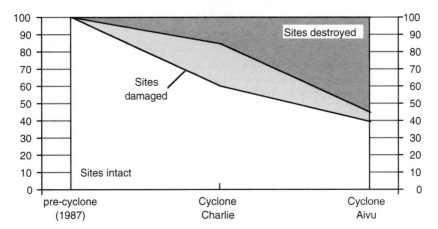

Figure 19.9. Survival of coastal midden sites after the cyclones 'Charlie' and 'Aivu' (data after Bird 1992).

Cultural resource management actions

The cultural resource management action comprised a survey of the area after the storm event and an assessment of the survival of the sites. As such then, this work is more detailed than that conducted in the previous case studies. The situation in Upstart Bay is fortuitous as a cyclone event had been preceded by a systematic site survey and all sites had been mapped. This then allowed a systematic investigation of the cyclone impact after each cyclone event. Apart from the removal of a threatened burial, which had occurred well before the cyclone events, no proactive management was undertaken. Sites had been recorded and on occasions sampled, but no systematic sampling and data recovery had been undertaken (Bird 1992).

Implications

Even though the data retrieval has been very limited, the cultural resource management actions taken give us an insight into the extent and speed of site decay and total site loss incurred as a result of tropical cyclones. As Bird (1992) has pointed out, the number of cyclones that hit the Queensland coast each year amounts, over time, to an exorbitant impact. If the devastation of cultural sites observed at Upstart Bay is any guide, the remaining - or surviving - archaeological record is more than impoverished.

Discussion

The three case studies have shown that ongoing coastal erosion poses a major threat to the conservation of cultural resources and that catastrophic events, such as cyclones, increase the impact significantly.

- The Marshall Islands site was only affected by a high pressure system and a higher than normal sea-level and greater current activity. As a result the erosion was 'gentle', exposing human remains and causing a sorting of these remains according to size classes with the lightweight bones being lost from the record.

- The Tongan example is similar, although caused by stronger storm surges. Again, an artifact sorting occurred, with much of the midden material washed away and any stratigraphy combined into a single artifact horizon. However, parts of the sites remain, and this is in part due to the reef platform extending from the islands, and the overall shallow nature of the beach profiles.

- In the North Queensland scenario, the beach profiles are steeper, and without the benefit of an adjacent reef platform, the storm surge is stronger and the erosive forces greater, leading to a total removal of the sites into the subtidal zone.

Geomorphological studies have shown that much of the island formation on coral atolls is due to cataclysmic events (Maragos *et al.* 1973) which, on the other hand, may destroy the entire island and all the cultural deposits on it (cf., Nadikdik Atoll in Spennemann & Marschner 1994). As the examples document, the variation of the impact depends not only on the strength of the event, but also, and significantly, on the subtidal topography of the shoreline. In addition, the frequency of the cyclones affects the long-term survival of sites, as cyclones may well occur so frequently that there is little chance of a replenishment of sediment, resulting in a net sediment loss and thus a rapid decay of the sites.

'Benefits' of storm surges

The destructive effects of cyclonic storm surges, and the mud and sand masses carried by them, must have had their effects throughout prehistory. At times, one effect was the archaeological preservation under the mudflows of the village destroyed by them. A good example is the site of Vaito'otia-Fa'ahia on Huahine in the Society Islands (Sinoto 1983a, 1983b). Similarly, at Anuta (Kirch 1982), a cyclonic storm surge apparently capped a prehistoric settlement with a roughly 0.5 m thick layer of sand, producing a hiatus in the occupation.

Low-intensity, continual erosion of beaches on Taroa Island, Maloelap Atoll, Marshall Islands, caused by current changes due to a World War II-period causeway, has gradually exposed a series of human remains, suggesting the presence of a cemetery nearby (Spennemann 1989b, 1990b). This was later found to be correct when an unmarked (and unrecorded) Japanese war cemetery adjacent to the shore was found after it had been vandalized by people looking for gold-filled teeth (Spennemann 1993b). In Fiji, cyclones frequently expose hitherto unknown archaeological deposits along the shoreline, so that monitoring the effects of cyclonic storm surges can be used as a 'surveying' technique (Clunie, F. 1986, pers. comm.). Unfortunately, however, this is only the 'poor cousin' of proper surveys (including auger surveys), as the sites thus found are usually destroyed or already severely impaired. The observations of Bird (1992) showed that large-scale cyclones were only destructive and did not expose hitherto unknown sites.

However, when assessing the actions we may wish to take, we need to consider both the likelihood and frequency, as well as strength of future hazards, and the constraints which act upon the mitigation options.

Implications of climatic change

One of the issues we need to consider are the implications posed by climatic change due to greenhouse gas-generated warming of the atmosphere and the related warming of the oceans. A rise in the atmospheric temperature and the sea surface temperature will generate climatic conditions favorable to more frequent and also more severe storms (Holland *et al.* 1988). As the sea surface temperature stands in direct correlation with the minimum sustainable pressure and hence intensity of tropical typhoons (Emanuel 1987), an increase in sea surface temperature, either during El Niño/Southern Oscillation (ENSO) events, or as a result of Greenhouse gas-induced global warming, is likely to (Wendland 1977):

- facilitate the occurrence of typhoons in areas hitherto not affected;

- shift the area of typhoon generation further eastward into the central Pacific;

- increase the frequency of storms and typhoons; and

- increase the severity of typhoons in areas already affected by typhoons.

Some of this can be observed today. The waters of the south-eastern equatorial Pacific Ocean undergo a quasi-cyclic phenomenon with a moving time interval of three to five years. During these effects, which have been termed the ENSO, global atmospheric disturbances develop. Based on an analysis of modern and historic data. Spennemann and Marschner (1994, 1995) have shown that the likelihood of a cyclone affecting the Marshall Islands during ENSO years is 2.6 times greater than during a non-ENSO year.

The implications of this then, are that cyclones will become an ever-increasing threat to the cultural resource base (Rowland 1992). However, as Murphy (1990) has shown, not all events of sea-level rise need result in the devastation of coastal sites by wave erosion. In his study of site 8SL-17, he found that the site, located on the backbeach of a sand cay, was covered by a sand dune system which did not erode during the Holocene rising sea-level, but was flooded, thus preserving *in situ* the archaeological site underneath.

Constraints on management options

Above we have established that archaeological sites located on low-lying, exposed islands are highly threatened by wave-generated erosion, through both occasional storm surges and day-to-day wave action. Further, it has been shown that the climate change in train is set to increase the threat on such sites. In order to preserve the richness of our cultural heritage, the protection of such sites is of importance. Since the conservation of these coastlines is almost always rendered impossible because of the horrendous costs involved or because the conservation action can in fact make matters worse (cf., Bird 1992 for Upstart Bay), it would appear that a sensible solution is that most of the threatened sites should be test-excavated as soon as possible in order to recover information. If the sampling shows the site's value, the majority of the site should be open for examination. Further, more detailed excavations should follow, wherever and whenever necessary.

However, the call to excavate is somewhat prescriptive and insensitive in view of issues such as these:

- traditional ownership of cultural resources;

- significance of the site to the traditional owners;

- advances in archaeological field and laboratory methodology.

Traditional ownership of cultural resources

Recent advances in cultural resource management in Australia (Frankel 1984) as well as the United States have taken the view that the indigenous population of the country needs to be consulted when it comes to site management options. Ethically speaking, ex-colonial powers hold little moral ownership and control over the heritage created by the people they conquered. Whilst the legal parameters governing control and management of cultural heritage may permit a number of actions, one should remember that these parameters were drawn up and defined by the 'powers-that-be' and only very rarely by those whose heritage is thus governed (Spennemann 1993a).

Significance of the site to the traditional owners

The requirement to consult with the traditional owners of the area following appropriate procedures is paramount if long-term management is to be successful (Spennemann & Look 1994). It needs to be considered that some of the management options, even though well-intended, may be deemed culturally inappropriate at best, and outright offensive at worst.

Advances in archaeological field and laboratory methodology

In past years, archaeological method and theory has advanced on a wide front and there is no reason to assume this will not continue. A vast array of tools has become available, ranging from optical dating to DNA analysis. Thus, it is prudent to leave sites in the ground, as they provide future generations of archaeologists with information hitherto inaccessible.

Implications

The above discussion has shown that cyclonic storm surges impact on shell middens and other coastal sites. From an archaeological viewpoint, abnormally strong wave action on the shoreline offers advantages and disadvantages. While wave action may expose hitherto unknown archaeological sites however, the negative impact of sites being washed away is greater. Thus, at first hand, excavation has some advantages in as much as some of the information contained in the sites can be collected and save. Yet, the excavation itself may not be an acceptable management option to the indigenous community. Site loss cannot be avoided - its impact on the level of heritage knowledge can only be minimized.

As the Queensland case study has shown, systematic survey of the coastal shell middens and other sites allows one to accurately assess the impact of cyclones on the middens. If the survey is accompanied with a representative sampling and/or auguring program (following consultation with, and consent by, the traditional owners) some of the data can be retrieved before the sites are devastated by the cyclones. The systematic resurvey of the area after the cyclone allows one to assess the extent of the erosion and site loss.

Cultural resource management should ensure that all sites are *regularly* monitored to ensure documentation of all sites and their changing fate over time. This allows one to project the observed site loss back into the past and so understand the changes the archaeological record may have undergone.

It is clear that appropriate level of management is a costly affair. Every time a cyclone strikes, the area affected by the storm surge and/or the winds, needs to be resurveyed. Ideally, the entire coastline affected by the cyclone would be resurveyed at regular intervals to monitor the gradual site erosion or site burial.

The case studies have shown that cyclones pose a major threat to the cultural heritage and that there is no easy solution.

Bibliography

Adams, William H., Ross, R. E. & Krause, E. L. (1990) 'Archaeological Survey of Taroa Island, Maloelap Atoll, Republic of the Marshall Islands', Report submitted to Micronesian Endowment for Historical Preservation, March 10, 1990, Report on file R.M.ii. Historic Preservation Office, Majuro.

Baan, G. van der (1977) 'Een onderzoek naar het anspoolen von shelpen I', *Het Zeepard*, 37: 94-96.

Baan, G., van der (1978a) 'Een onderzoek naar het anspoolen von shelpen II', *Het Zeepard*, 38: 5-9.

Baan, G., van der (1978b) 'Een onderzoek naar het anspoolen von shelpen III', *Het Zeepard*, 38: 34-39.

Bird, E. C. F. (1984) *Coasts: An introduction to coastal geomorphology*, 3rd edition, Australian National University Press, Canberra.

Bird, M. K. (1992) 'The impact of tropical cyclones on the archaeological record: an Australian example', *Archaeology in Oceania*, 27: 75-86.

Blumenstock, D. I. (ed.) (1961) 'A report on Typhoon effects upon Jaluit Atoll', *Atoll Research Bulletin 75*, Pacific Science Board, Washington DC.

Cooper, Z. (1985) 'Archaeological explorations in the Andaman Islands', *Bulletin of the Indo-Pacific Prehistory Association*, 6: 27-39.

Emanuel, K. A. (1987) 'The dependence of hurricane intensity on climate', *Nature*, 326: 483-485.

Frankel, D. (1984) 'Who owns the past?' *Australian Society*, 3 (9): 14-15.

Gjeesing, F. C. & Tyson, G. F. (1990) *Report on hurricane Hugo's impact on historical resources in the US Virgin Islands*, St. Thomas Historical Trust and St. Croix Landmarks Society, US Virgin Islands.

Holland, G. J., McBride, J. L. & Nicholls, N. (1988) 'Australian region cyclones and the greenhouse effect', *in Greenhouse. Planning for a climatic change*, ed. G. I. Pearman, E. J. Brill, London, pp. 438-456.

Hopley, D. (1974b) 'Coastal changes produced by tropical cyclone 'Althea' in Queensland', December 1971, *Australian Geographer*, 12: 462-468.

Hopley, D. & Harvey, N. (1979) 'Regional variation in storm surge characteristics around the Australian coast: a preliminary investigation', in *Natural hazards in Australia*, eds R. L. Heathcote & B. G. Thom, Australian Academy of Science, Canberra.

Hughes, P. J. & Sullivan, M. E. (1974) 'The re-deposition of midden material by storm waves', *Journal and Proceedings of the Royal Society of New South Wales*, 107: 6-10.

Kirch, P. V. (1982) 'A revision of the Anuta sequence', *Journal of the Polynesian Society*, 91: 245-254.

Lever, J., Van Den Bosh, M., Cook, H., Van Dijk, T., Thiadens, A. J. K. & Thijssen, R. (1964) 'Quantitative beach research II: An experiment with artificial valves of *Donax vittatus*', *Netherlands Journal of Sea Geology*, 2(3): 458-492.

Lilley, I. (1986) Prehistoric Exchange in the Vitiaz Strait, New Guinea, PhD thesis, Australian National University, Canberra, unpub.

Maragos, J., Baines, J. B. K. & Beveridge, P. (1973) 'Tropical cyclone creates new land formation on Funafuti Atoll', *Science*, 181: 161-164.

Meehan, B. (1982) *From shellbed to shellmidden*, Australian Institute of Aboriginal Studies, Canberra.

Murphy, L. (1990) '8SL-17: Natural Site Formation processes of a multiple-component underwater site in Florida', *Southwest Cultural Resources Center Professional Papers*, No. 39. Santa Fe, New Mexico.

Nelson, C. L. (1991) *Protecting the Past from Natural Disasters*, The Preservation Press, Washington, DC.

Oliver, J. & Reardon, G. F. (1982) 'Tropical Cyclone Isaac. Cyclonic impact in the context of the society and economy of the Kingdom of Tonga', *Disaster Investigation Report No. 5*, Townsville: Centre for Disaster Studies, James Cook University of North Queensland.

Rowland, M. J. (1992) 'Climate change, sea-level rise and the archaeological record', *Australian Archaeology*, 34: 29-33.

Sinoto, Y. H. (1983a) 'Huahine: heritage of the great navigators', *Museum*, 137: 70-73.

Sinoto, Y. H. (1983b) 'The Huahine excavation: discovery of an ancient Polynesian canoe', *Archaeology*, 36:10-15.

Spennemann, D. H. R. (1986) 'The impact of cyclonic surge on archaeological sites: a case study from some low-lying islands off Tongatapu, Kingdom of Tonga', Report prepared for the Ministry of Lands, Surveys and Natural Resources, and for the Tonga Traditions Committee, Nuku'alofa, Kingdom of Tonga, Manuscript on file, Ministry of Lands, Surveys and Natural Resources, Nuku'alofa, Kingdom of Tonga.

Spennemann, D. H. R. (1987) 'The impact of cyclonic surge on archaeological sites in Tonga', *Bulletin of the Indo-Pacific Prehistory Association*, 7: 75-87.

Spennemann, D. H. R. (1989a) `ata `a Tonga mo `ata `o Tonga: Early and Later *Prehistory of the Tongan Islands*, PhD thesis, Department of Prehistory, Research School of Pacific Studies, The Australian National University, Canberra (University Microfilms International).

Spennemann, D. H. R. (1989b) 'Report on a human femur from the south-western coast of Tõrwa Island, Maloelap Atoll, Republic of the Marshall Islands', Osteological Report DRS 52 (1989), Manuscript on file, Alele Museum, Majuro, Republic of the Marshall Islands, 4 pp.

Spennemann, D. H. R. (1990a) 'Eroding cemeteries in the D-U-D area. Report on a brief survey to determine the extent of coastal erosion on the ocean side of Jarõj, Wülka and Telap Islands, Majuro Atoll, Republic of the Marshall Islands', Geomorphological Report DRS-GEO 5 (1990), Report prepared for the Historic Preservation Office, Majuro, Republic of the Marshall Islands.

Spennemann, D. H. R. (1990b) 'Report on a human ulna from the south-eastern coast of Tõrwa Island, Maloelap Atoll, Republic of the Marshall Islands', Report presented to the Historic Preservation Office, Majuro, Republic of the Marshall Islands (1990), Report OTIA-TAG-MAR-42-7/90, 4 pp.

Spennemann, D. H. R. (1990c) 'Osteological analysis of human remains from site MI-Mj-242 found at Laura Beach, Majuro Island (Laura), Majuro Atoll, Republic of the Marshall Islands', Osteological Report DRS 54 (1990), Report presented to the Historic Preservation Office, Majuro, Republic of the Marshall Islands.

Spennemann, D. H. R. (1990d) 'Report on part of a human cranium from Bwuron Island, Majuro Atoll, Republic of the Marshall Islands', Osteological Report DRS 56 (1990), Report presented to the Historic Preservation Office, Majuro, Republic of the Marshall Islands, HPO Report No. 2 - 1990, Manuscript on file, Historic Preservation Office, Majuro, Republic of the Marshall Islands.

Spennemann, D. H. R. (1991) 'Selektion menschlicher Skelettreste in ausgewaschenen Grabstätten: eine Fallstudie von den Marshall-Inseln', *Archäologische Informationen*, 14(1): 32-40.

Spennemann, D. H. R. (1992a) 'Differential representation of human skeletal remains in eroded and redeposited coastal deposits: A case study from the Marshall Islands', *International Journal of Anthropology*, 7(1): 1-8.

Spennemann, D. H. R. (1992b) *Cultural Resource Management Plan for Majuro Atoll, Republic of the Marshall Islands*, US Department of Interior, Office of Territorial and International Affairs, Washington, 2 vols.

Spennemann, D. H. R. (1993a) 'Multicultural Resources Management - a Pacific Perspective', *Historic Preservation Forum*, 7(1): 20-26.

Spennemann, D. H. R. (1993b) 'Observations of Vandalism at a Japanese Cemetery on Taroa Island, Maloelap Atoll', HPO-Report 1993/1, Majuro Atoll, Historic Preservation Office, Republic of the Marshall Islands.

Spennemann, D. H. R. (1993c) 'Toorlok Bok. Predictions of environmental, economical, social and cultural impacts of a potential rise in relative sea-level on the atolls of the Marshall Islands, in Climate Change: Implications for Natural Resource Conservation, *Occasional Papers in Biological Sciences 1*, University of Western Sydney, Hawkesbury, pp. 185-251.

Spennemann, D. H. R. (1994) *Physical Conservation Techniques*, Modular external study package for undergraduate course PKM 368, Open Learning Institute, Charles Sturt University, Wagga Wagga.

Spennemann, D. H. R., Bigler, C. & Anjain, A. (1992) 'Cultural Resource Management in the Republic of the Marshall Islands 90/91', *ISLA - Journal of Micronesian Studies*, 1(2): 437-444.

Spennemann, D. H. R., Byrne, G. & Belz, L. H. (1990) 'An outline of the potential impacts of greenhouse gas generated climatic change and projected sea-level rise on Tongatapu, Kingdom of Tonga. With special emphasis on the Nuku'alofa township area', in *Implications of expected climate changes in the South Pacific region: an overview. United Nations Environmental Programme Regional Seas Reports & Studies Series*, eds G. Pernetta & P. J. Hughes, 128: 161-192.

Spennemann, D. H. R. & Look, D. W. (1994) 'Writing Conservation Management Plans. Concepts and Considerations for Conservation Management Plans', in *Conservation Management of Historic Metal in Tropical Environments. Background Notes*, eds D. W. Look & D. H. R. Spennemann, No. 11. Charles Sturt University, Albury, Australia and US National Park Service, Western Regional Office, San Francisco, CA.

Spennemann, D. H. R. & Marschner, I. G. (1994) 'Stormy Years. On the association between the El Niño/Southern oscillation phenomenon and the occurrence of typhoons in the Marshall Islands' *Johnstone Centre Report No. 9*, The Johnstone Centre, Charles Sturt University, Albury.

Spennemann, D. H. R. & Marschner, I. G. (1995) 'Association between ENSO and typhoons in the Marshall Islands', *Disasters*, 19(3): 194-197.

Stoddart, D. R. (1975) 'Sand cays of Tongatapu', *Atoll Research Bulletin 181*, Smithsonian Institution, Washington DC.

US Army Corps of Engineers (1989) *Majuro Atoll Coastal Resource Atlas*, US Army Corps of Engineers, Pacific Ocean Division, Honolulu HI.

Wendland, W. M. (1977) 'Tropical storm frequencies related to sea surface temperatures', *Journal of Applied Meteorology*, 16: 477-481.

Woodroffe, C. D. (1983) 'The impact of cyclone Isaac on the coast of Tonga', *Pacific Science*, 37: 181-210.

Zallar, S. A., Siow, K. & Coutts, P. J. F. (1979) *Stabilisation of coastal archaeological sites in Victoria - A pilot study*, Ministry for Conservation Victoria, Melbourne.

Barksdale, Daryl (1998) 'Disaster recovery response to
Tropical Storm Alberto', in *Disaster Management
Programs for Historic Sites*, eds Dirk H. R. Spennemann
& David W. Look. San Francisco and Albury: Associa-
tion for Preservation Technology (Western Chapter) and
The Johnstone Centre, Charles Sturt University. Pp. 133-
138.

20

Disaster recovery response to Tropical Storm Alberto

DARYL BARKSDALE [¶]

Tropical Storm Alberto hit the State of Georgia in July 1994 and, as a result, about a third of our state suffered flood and rain damage. Fifty-five of the 160+ counties of Georgia had been declared federal disaster counties. Most of the damage was concentrated in the south-western part of the state, especially along the Flint River.

Recovery program

The recovery efforts included administering a US$2.475 million flood recovery grant program; coordinating with the National Trust for Historic Preservation, the Georgia Trust and other state agencies in comprehensive relief efforts; and working with the Federal Emergency Management Agency (FEMA) in the National Historic Preservation Act Section 106 review process. The Georgia program is similar to the relief programs in the State of California and in the Midwest. Funding is designed for the repair of historic properties that 'fall through the cracks' - that is, that do not receive money from FEMA or from private insurance. The Georgia Historic Preservation Division currently has seventy grant projects in place that are aiding over one hundred historic structures and archaeological sites. We are repairing public buildings like courthouses, private residences, commercial buildings and museums.

Recovery experiences

The Georgia State Historic Preservation Officer (SHPO) had no past experience in disaster response. This flood was a 500-year disaster for Georgia, and is considered the worst natural disaster in Georgia's recorded history. The Georgia Historic Preservation Division

---

[¶] Flood Assistance Coordinator, Georgia Historic Preservation Division, Department of Natural Resources, 205 Butler Street, SE, Suite 1462, Atlanta, GA 30334, USA

was organized and quick in its response efforts, and also fortunate that it could call the National Trust for Historic Preservation and the Midwest State Historic Preservation Officers for guidance.

Figure 20.1. Aerial view of the 1920s Radium Springs Casino, Albany, Georgia, inundated by floods in July 1994. (Photo: Jim Lockhart 1994).

This provided for a head start on which steps to take and which to avoid. The Georgia SHPO was also able to access FEMA's Programmatic Agreement from the Midwest and adapt it quickly for the state.

One of the first hurdles we had to overcome in recovery work was lack of documentation. The flooded areas were for the most part rural and over a large area and there was little survey work or National Register listings in these areas. This made organized damage assessment difficult. Compensation came from information provided by regional preservation planners, main street directors and local government contacts. Often this information was not on paper or on a computer.

It was beneficial to go into the field with representatives of other state agencies. This was beneficial not only to the SHPO, but to the disaster victims as well, since the information presented was coordinated. The Governor's Office of Georgia formed an interagency flood recovery team that included Historic Preservation Division, FEMA, the Georgia Emergency Management Agency and other state agencies. The team visited different cities in the state and discussed the Historic Preservation Division's flood recovery grants, the US Small Business Administration loans, FEMA aid and the application procedure for the aid. Packets were handed out so that the information was delineated for them.

Figure 20.2. The Radium Springs Casino in 1996, following the restoration. A US$ 57,000 grant by the Georgia Historic Preservation Division assisted in the recovery (Photo: Jim Lockhart 1996).

During Georgia's recovery efforts, it has become apparent that technical information and education is crucial before, during and after a disaster. Historic material was lost because disaster victims did not know how to deal with water damage to their resources. Often this occurred immediately after the disaster, before technical information could reach them. A chronic problem that existed was the failure of building owners to allow their structures to dry out before repair and replacement; as a result, the work often had to be redone. The Georgia Historic Preservation Division is currently planning, in coordination with the Alabama State Historic Preservation Officer, technical information workshops in the flood areas for architects, building inspectors and home owners in the flood regions, so that they will have better knowledge in the future. As part of our grant administration, we have hired two contract architects to aid grant recipients in this area. Our architects live in the flood regions, and they provide assistance with every part of the repair process.

Montezuma, Georgia

Montezuma has a population of about 4,500. It is a flood town in Georgia and is a good example of how historic preservation and disaster recovery can work; the recovery efforts here are still in progress. In July 1994, Montezuma received 20 inches (50 cm) of rain in 24 hours; the breaking of the levee bank resulted in the entire downtown of Montezuma being underwater.

Figure 20.3. Historic home in Albany, Georgia, following Tropical Storm Alberto in July 1994. The flood waters washed out part of the foundation all causing the collapse of the wooden structure (Photo: Jim Lockhart 1996).

This town has been very focused on taking advantage of the resources that are available and has been receptive to historic preservation and understand its advantages. The people of Montezuma have learned a lot about preservation since the flood.

All the buildings downtown are privately-owned commercial buildings with no flood insurance. The first step the merchants took was to apply for Small Business Administration loans so that they could re-open their businesses. They next sought grant money from the Georgia Historic Preservation Division. Since the entire Central Business District in Montezuma was underwater, we were able to give the city a block grant for facade repair. This grant gave us a chance to provide comprehensive improvement to an entire commercial district.

There are about 45 buildings in downtown Montezuma that are contributing to a potential National Register District. The National Register Nomination is presently being completed.

Many of the facades have extensive brick and structural damage resulting from the flood. The block grant will repair this type of damage, but beyond this, the town is interested in going one step further with about five buildings downtown. The non-historic aluminum facades will be removed to expose the original intact facades underneath.

Beyond this, the town is also taking advantage of aid from the National Trust for Historic Preservation and the Georgia Trust. They are both offering to help the town with economic development, heritage tourism and other incentives. Historic Preservation Division's Certified Local Government coordinator is working with them to implement appropriate zoning and to obtain Certified Local Government status.

Figure 20.4. Aerial view of the Commercial Area of downtown Montezuma, Georgia, inundated by floods following Tropical Storm Alberto in July 1994. (Photo: Jim Lockhart 1996).

Figure 20.5. Conservation management action following the flooding of Montezuma, Georgia, allowed the rehabilitation of the damaged structures. A façade rehabilitation block grant allowed the restoration of historic structures and the removal of metal slipcover on commercial buildings. (Photo: Jim Lockhart 1996).

Figure 20.6. Following the flooding by Tropical Storm Alberto of Montezuma, Georgia, the city was the recipient of a US$ 600,000 Flood Recovery Grant to rehabilitate over 40 commercial buildings.   (Photo: Jim Lockhart 1997).

All of this activity in Montezuma is a result of flood recovery efforts. This town is an example of how preservation benefits flood recovery, and how Georgia's Historic Preservation Division recovery program is succeeding.

Baldrica, Alice M. (1998) 'Flood case study: Stillwater,
Nevada', in *Disaster Management Programs for Historic
Sites*, eds Dirk H. R. Spennemann & David W. Look.
San Francisco and Albury: Association for Preservation
Technology (Western Chapter) and The Johnstone
Centre, Charles Sturt University. Pp. 139-142.

21

Flood case study: Stillwater, Nevada

ALICE M. BALDRICA [¶]

Nevada is a desert and the driest state in the union. Its evaporation rate usually exceeds its precipitation rate. Following a lengthy drought in the 1970s, northern Nevada enjoyed three years of above average precipitation. Between 1982 and 1984, both the Humboldt and Carson Rivers emptied enormous amounts of water into the Humboldt Basin and Carson Sink (all rivers save two in Nevada empty into interior basins rather than drain into an ocean). To save farms and homes in the Lovelock community along the Humboldt, state agencies breached a natural dike between the Humboldt Basin and Carson Sink.

This action flooded the Carson Sink. Excess water flowed from the Humboldt and other drainages into the Carson Sink, the lowest point in northwestern Nevada - below 39,360 feet (1,200 m) in elevation. The Carson Sink contains the Stillwater Marsh that is important habitat for waterfowl. In prehistoric times, the marsh probably contained 79,000 acres (31,600 ha) of fresh water. In 1982, prior to spring runoff, the marsh had stood at an all-time low of 8,500 acres (3,400 ha) of water. By the summer of 1984, over 220,000 acres (88,000 ha) were flooded. The vegetation in the marshes died; so did the fish and the birds. Dikes were breached, nesting areas vanished.

The flooding also affected hundreds of prehistoric archaeological sites within the marsh. The Stillwater Marsh is a National Register District located 10 miles (16.1 km) northeast of Fallon, a community in northwestern Nevada. The US Fish and Wildlife Service manages this area of the Carson Sink as the Stillwater Wildlife Management Area. The archaeological district encompasses almost 42,000 acres (16,800 ha). Little was known about the area when it was nominated to the National Register of Historic Places in 1975 other than that 'Indian campsites' were present. The Register nomination describes the presence of "arrowheads, grinding stones, beads and other artifacts". In 1975, the US

[¶] Archaeologist, Nevada State Historic Preservation Office, Nevada State Historic Preservation Office, 100 South Stewart Street, Capitol Complex, Carson City, Nevada 89710, USA

Fish and Wildlife Service was unaware of any burials (Stillwater Marsh National Register Nomination). By 1982, archaeologists had recorded approximately 85 sites in this archaeological district but this information was based on surface survey. Archaeologists did not know what lay beneath the surface.

In 1986, the flood water began to recede. US Fish and Wildlife Service employees began to note the appearance of human bones on exposed ground in the marsh and contacted the State Historic Preservation Office. Over 45 new archaeological sites and over 125 burials were uncovered as the water evaporated. These sites averaged 246 feet (75 m) by 131 feet (40 m) and contained a dense scattering of archaeological materials: flaked stone, ground stone, fire cracked rock, clam shells, animal bones, human burials, house floors, cache pits and midden. For the most part, the sites were located on what had been islands in the marsh in prehistoric times (Fagan & Raymond 1987, pp. 27-28). The find was unprecedented and unexpected in the Great Basin. Open stratified sites in this number and density had not been discovered in northern Nevada prior to 1986. These sites had not been visible previously. They had stood under 7.8 inches (20 cm) to 19.5 inches (50 cm) of sediments prior to flooding. So invisible were they that numerous archaeological surveys in the area during the 1970s failed to reveal their presence.

Impacts

The sites were heavily impacted. Firstly, wind and wave action had stripped 7.8 inches (20 cm) to 19.5 inches (50 cm) of sediments from the sites that had existed on islands within the marsh. Waves mechanically eroded sites, particularly those with northern and western exposures. During the winter, wind-driven ice scoured the edges of sites. The heavy mineral content of the water saturated both human and animal bone, corroding them beyond recognition as soon as they were exposed at the surface (Fagan & Raymond 1987, pp. 38-45). Exposure of artifacts left the sites vulnerable to pot hunters who sought to collect relics and skeletons as trophies.

Immediate effects to response

The federal agency was immediately hampered by a lack of personnel. Only five full-time employees, none of them archaeologists, managed the 163,000 acre (65,200 hectares) management area. They also lacked information about the exact location of sites and the nature of sites. Another factor hampering response was access. Some sites were accessible only by airboats which were few in number at the reserve. Funding for site treatment also was not available. Fish and Wildlife Service employees at the management area contacted the State soon after they realized they could not manage the situation.

The US Fish and Wildlife Service did manage to come up with about US$10,000 to fund a 'salvage plan' with the consent of the State Historic Preservation Officer and the Advisory Council on Historic Preservation. Given the small amount of funds, the agency relied on state archaeologists from the State Historic Preservation Officer, the Nevada State Museum and Nevada Department of Transportation as well as the director of the Churchill County museum and local volunteers to recover burials exposed more than 50% or that were not in original context, exposed animal bone at sites and artifacts that might prove attractive to relic collectors. Such artifacts included portable grindstones and projectile points. The US Fish and Wildlife Service provided the transportation, by airboat. These were considered temporary measures until Fish and Wildlife Service could obtain additional funding. The Nevada State Museum staff cataloged, analyzed and curated the artifacts.

Damage occurred where sites had already eroded completely or corrosion of bone had already taken place. Pot hunters were one step ahead of archaeologists in many places. The long-term management of the archaeological district was still a problem.

Long-term recovery

After this initial data recovery, the US Fish and Wildlife Service faced two major tasks. One was to re-establish the marsh through repair of structures and revegetation. The other was the stabilization and protection of archaeological sites. The agency sought to collapse these into a single program but it needed to know more about the nature of the environment and the nature of the archaeology. Funding would have presented an insurmountable obstacle except for the attention the archaeological finds received. Interested members of the public and agency archaeologists kept the media informed about events at the Marsh, the marvelous nature of the finds, their importance to the local tribe and the threats presented by erosion and pot hunters. Letters to Nevada's congressional delegation helped place money where it was needed. The health of the marsh and the protection of archaeological sites were linked in this effort.

In 1987, the agency hired an archaeologist to work exclusively at the Stillwater Wildlife Management Area, to perform certain tasks agreed on by US Fish and Wildlife Service, the Nevada State Historic Preservation Officer and the Advisory Council on Historic Preservation. The archaeologist began by creating a database, accurately mapping and recording each known site in the management area. The US Army Corps of Engineers developed an action plan for stabilizing and protecting sites (Fagan & Raymond 1987). To understand the structure of the sites and develop a context for evaluating their research value, the agency contracted with a private consulting firm to conduct test excavations (Raven & Elston 1988). With the accumulation of this data, the US Fish and Wildlife Service was able to rank sites according to their ability to answer research questions and on immediate threats such as wind based erosion and relic collection. This allowed the Fish and Wildlife Service to set priorities for data recovery and other forms of treatment.

Implementation of the plan to re-establish the marsh and protect archaeological sites involved construction. The agency constructed new dikes and wave barriers around sites. Artificial nesting islands were constructed on the windward side of existing islands to serve as wind and water barriers to protect sites. Roads to vulnerable sites were closed. Priority was given to the revegetation of sites using shallow rooting plants to stabilize the soil.

At the same time, the US Fish and Wildlife Service initiated an ethnographic study to determine the kinds of resources and sites important to the Northern Paiute who inhabited the area (Fowler 1992). The agency also consulted with the Fallon Paiute-Shoshone Tribe to determine the disposition of the burials resulting in a memorandum of understanding. The recovered burials are interred in a crypt overlooking the marsh, secure from pot hunters. It is opened every few years to inter additional burials or human remains that have eroded out of sites within the Marsh.

The National Park Service funded the development of a plan for the treatment of archaeological sites for both the Humboldt Basin and Carson Sink. The plan, drawing on work conducted by the US Fish and Wildlife Service and its consultants, identified research issues of importance to the area as a whole. The plan identifies significant sites and the data necessary to address important research questions (Elston, Raven & Baldrica 1992).

Preparedness

We know that flooding is likely to happen again; we know that these sites remain vulnerable. Excavation of all sites is impractical. The cost of data recovery is prohibitively high and the Fallon Paiute-Shoshone Tribe would prefer to see burials remain in place. However, US Fish and Wildlife Service and the State of Nevada are better prepared than we were in 1986. Maps and site records are on file at the Refuge and at the Nevada State Museum. Relationships with locals, the state and the tribe are in place, and the agency has a familiarity with the process to care for its cultural resources. We will be ready when flooding occurs again.

Bibliography

Elston, Robert G., Christopher Raven & Alice M. Baldrica (1992) *Prehistoric Wetlands Adaptations in the Carson Desert and the Humboldt Sink. An Element of the Nevada State Historic Preservation Plan*, State of Nevada, Carson City, Nevada.

Fagan, John & Anan Raymond (1987) *Plan of Action for Cultural Resource Management at Stillwater Wildlife Management Area*, US Army Corps of Engineers, Portland District, Oregon.

Fowler, Catherine S. (1992) 'In the Shadow of Fox Peak', *US Fish and Wildlife Service, Region 1, Cultural Resource Series No. 5*, Washington, DC.

Raven, Christopher & Robert Elston (eds) (1988) Preliminary Investigations in Stillwater Marsh: Human Prehistory and Geoarchaeology, Vols 1 & 2. *US Fish and Wildlife Service, Region 1, Cultural Resource Series No. 1*, Washington, DC.

Stillwater Marsh National Register nomination (n.d.) On file at the Nevada State Historic Preservation Office, Carson City, Nevada.

TERRORIST ATTACK

Osborne, E. (1998) 'Disaster Response for the Oklahoma City Bombing',in *Disaster Management Programs for Historic Sites*, eds Dirk H. R. Spennemann & David W. Look. San Francisco and Albury: Association for Preservation Technology (Western Chapter) and The Johnstone Centre, Charles Sturt University. Pp. 145-148.

22
Disaster response for the Oklahoma City bombing

EVA OSBORNE [¶]

As a result of the explosion at the Alfred P. Murrah Federal Building 19 April 1995, many properties of historical significance to the Oklahoma City community were damaged. The State Historic Preservation Office (SHPO) was located in the Journal Record Building, an historic building immediately north of the Murrah Building. The office was temporarily relocated, without office equipment, files or supplies, and some of the staff were hospitalized due to injuries sustained during the bombing. Although we had minimal resources of our own, our goal was to work with the City of Oklahoma City to assist the property owners within the bomb-affected area by assessing the damage to each historic building and offering direction for the steps they could take to repair and preserve their properties.

We consulted with the National Park Service, the National Trust, the Federal Emergency Management Agency (FEMA) and the American Institute of Architects to assemble teams consisting of preservation experts, architects and structural engineers who worked on a volunteer basis to produce written reports for individual properties based on site visits during the week of 15-19 May 1995. Coincidentally, Oklahoma's Seventh Annual Statewide Preservation Conference had been scheduled for the first week of May in Oklahoma City at a building a few blocks south of the Murrah Building. We used this forum as a gathering place for our preservation partners who came to assist, to inform the public about the extent of the damage and to introduce information and sources for information concerning preservation of these buildings.

[¶] Historic Preservation Architect, State Historic Preservation Office, 2704 Villa Prom, Shepherd Mall, Oklahoma City, OK 73107, USA

After relocating, acquiring telephone service and securing administrative assistance with computers, etc., we defined the disaster area on a map and subdivided this area into zones of similar types of expected damage. Seventy-three National Register eligible buildings were identified; statistical information concerning current property owners and addresses was collected; and early reports about building damage by FEMA, various insurance companies and the City were collected. The State of Oklahoma, Department of Central Services, Risk Management Division (also located in the Journal Record Building) provided handouts with a checklist for immediate stabilization and updated telephone numbers for utility companies, and disaster assistance agencies. Information about emergency response for various recent natural disasters was studied and consolidated. The General Service Administration provided us with a chart to record specific information about damage. This chart was used as a model system for recording data by our damage assessment team. All of this information was adapted to our particular needs and organized in three-ring binders with schedules, locations and contacts for team members and general preservation information to refresh the memories of our volunteer professionals of currently recommended preservation practice. The Secretary of the Interior's Standards for Rehabilitation and the National Park Service's brochure explaining the 20% tax credit for certified historic structures were key tools for encouraging appropriate rehabilitation.

Figure #.1 The Alfred P. Murrah Federal Building after the bombing on 19 April 1995

All affected National Register eligible properties were of concern. However, because of the immediacy of the situation, we prioritized 19 properties and one proposed historic district, each with special historical significance and/or reported severe damage. Our teams were divided into four groups corresponding with four building types: civic buildings, religious buildings, small businesses and large commercial buildings. A cumulative damage assessment report was presented to the Oklahoma City, City Council and individual assessment reports with recommendations and general preservation material were given to each property owner. This report was intended to be used as 'a second set of eyes' to supplement private insurance reports and to offer property owners hope that their buildings could be rehabilitated rather than demolished, as well as provide our best available sources about how to accomplish this goal. Later feedback showed that this report was used for a wide variety of unexpected purposes.

The National Park Service sent staff historical architects and structural engineers, and the National Trust contracted a structural engineer with preservation and disaster recovery experience, each assigned to a team. These preservation professionals wrote concluding remarks for each of the building types as well as summaries of the type of damage that they observed. All statements focused attention toward rehabilitation/restoration in an effort to counter the temptation to raze the buildings and build anew. Considerable effort was given to working with the City concerning code issues. We were fortunate that there was adequate federal funding for reimbursement for documented damage, as well as new construction that would bring the buildings into compliance with current code. However, discussions concerning potential problems planted the seed for consideration of new building codes that allow sensitivity to historic fabric to be adopted in the future. Our report addressed all issues short of actual cost estimates.

Figure #.2. The city center of Oklahoma City after the bombing. The Alfred P. Murrah Federal Building is located in the left foreground.

The members of the federal agencies on each of the teams were frequently asked by the media and various construction management organizations to address questions concerning estimated costs for repair. Questions concerning individual properties were directed to property owners and their insurance companies as appropriate and estimates for total damage were referred to FEMA.

Typical damage observed by our team was caused by a variety of forces. The explosion was like the winds of a tornado in respect to single directional lateral forces and positive and negative air pressure pockets expressed primarily in the loss of window glazing within a large area of the bombing site. Several of the churches were left with misaligned pitched roofing systems after the roof was picked up and dropped into its new position. The ground shook with waves of force like that experienced in an earthquake causing steel structural systems to move harmonically as the buildings lost masonry veneer systems, interior partitions and, in some cases, connections primarily at upper floor and roofing joists. Damage typical to floods including future problems with saturated masonry, mold and parasites, etc. was initiated by fire sprinkler systems responding to the blast by saturating the interiors of the buildings during evacuation, and additional water damage occurred in numerous buildings that remained open to the elements during the following months. The team was constantly amazed at the unpredictable and seemingly irrational patterns of damage and movement that extended 30 miles in three directions.

Evacuation was impaired by twisted suspended ceiling carcasses lining the corridors like barbed wire. Fire stair egress doors were blocked by debris at ground level because the doors swing out into the areas of damage instead of in toward the relatively clear fire stair landing. In the Journal Record Building, the congestion of people pushing outward on the door was not a problem until well after the first person found the door inoperable.

This disaster differs from the natural disasters discussed in previous presentations in that it was an intentional act of violence, directed at a specific target. The target was the government who typically acts as the avenue of assistance rather than the victim. The site was immediately roped off after evacuation and labeled a "crime scene" controlled by the FBI. All access in and out, including collected information or photographs describing the condition of the site, were screened. The lengthy process of collecting evidence took precedence over stabilization of the area. The terrifying nature of this incident attracted worldwide attention and an immediate national response. Public promises concerning reimbursement, recovery and justice came from high places, in many cases, prior to any realistic plan for fulfilling the promise. After the emergency response and stabilization of the area, those affected must begin the long process of rebuilding, in some cases, with the expectation that this can occur at an accelerated rate. The resulting frustration could be minimized by clearly defining areas of authority, processing written information concerning services and requirements for receiving these services, and making sure that this information is distributed to everyone concerned from a single source.

COMMUNICATION AND TRAINING

Spennemann, Dirk H. R. (1998) 'Natural disaster
mitigation and cultural heritage: a course proposal', in
Disaster Management Programs for Historic Sites, eds
Dirk H. R. Spennemann & David W. Look. San
Francisco and Albury: Association for Preservation
Technology (Western Chapter) and The Johnstone
Centre, Charles Sturt University. Pp. 151-164.

23

Natural disaster mitigation and cultural heritage: a course proposal

DIRK H. R. SPENNEMANN [¶]

This paper proposes the development of a tertiary education course 'Natural Disaster
Mitigation and Cultural Heritage' designed to develop common ground between the disaster
mitigation agencies on the one hand and the cultural heritage managers on the other. The
course, to be taught solely in distance education mode, is designed as a stand-alone unit,
both a professional development course and as a subject in a disaster management course.

The need for a course

Every natural disaster has an impact on the built environment: many buildings and
structures are affected, while some are damaged to a varied degree. The demolition,
however, is not confined to the disaster effect, but extends to the impact of the disaster
managers as well. The aftermath of the Loma Prieta Earthquake has shown that many
heritage buildings had been 'red-tagged', declared to be unsafe and were subsequently
demolished as a public safety exercise. In most cases, little or no assessment of their
historic significance had been carried out and little effort made to find means to conserve
and restore these sites (Nelson 1991). In many cases, developers and some property
owners actively seized upon the opportunity to rid themselves of heritage-listed properties.
An almost identical scenario, albeit on a smaller scale, was played out in Newcastle,
Australia (Henry 1991).

[¶] The Johnstone Centre, Charles Sturt University, PO Box 789, Albury NSW 2640, Australia.
E-mail: dspennemann@csu.edu.au

It has been asserted many times by numerous speakers at the symposium that there is substantial need for public education and that the parties involved in disaster mitigation efforts should have the appropriate skills and an understanding of the major issues and procedures of cultural heritage management.

Other disaster management courses

A number of universities, both in the United States and Canada as well as in Australia, offer disaster management courses, either as full-length tertiary courses or as single subjects and professional development course units. These courses focus on the common training needs, such as disaster relief, hazard reduction, human resource management and the like. A compilation by the Natural Hazards Center in Colorado (Blanchard 1995) lists the following providers for the Americas (Table 22.1).

Table 22.1. Disaster management course providers in the Americas

Canada
University of British Columbia

United States of America	
Arkansas State University	St. Petersburg College
California Specialized Training Institute	Tennessee Technological University
California State University, Long Beach	Texas A & M University
California State University, Los Angeles	Texas Tech University
California State University, Chico	The City University of New York
California State University, Fullerton	The Graduate School of America
Cincinnati Technical College	Thomas Edison State College
Clark University	University of California at Berkeley
Eastern Michigan University	University of Colorado
Florida State University	University of Delaware
Front Range Community College	University of Denver
Frontier Community College	University of Houston
Garland County Community College	University of Kansas
George Washington University	University of Maryland
Georgia State University	University of Massachusetts
Hampton University	University of Miami
Indiana Public Safety Training Institute	University of Michigan-Flint
Lewis and Clark Community College	University of North Texas
New Mexico State University	University of South Carolina
Pennsylvania State University	University of Southern California
Red Rocks Community College	University of Toledo
Rochester Institute of Technology	University of Utah
Saint Joseph's University	University of Wisconsin
Southern Illinois University	Washington University

In addition, the following providers for Australia need to be considered:

- Associate Diploma of Emergency Management (University of Tasmania)
- University of New England
- Queensland University

Whilst some of the cultural resource management needs are addressed in passing in some of the units making up these courses, none of these courses dedicate a *full* subject (unit) to the needs of cultural heritage resources. It is evident then, that the common course offerings do not address the safeguards of cultural heritage resources. As a result there is an information gap, which leads to the disregard of cultural resources in the event of natural disasters and there is a potential for conflict. A good avenue to reduce the level of conflict is to facilitate the communication between the conflicting stakeholders. This can be achieved by the provision of a fully accredited university-level training course.

The professional development market

The market for such a course consists of both disaster management professionals and cultural heritage managers. The following categories of professionals form the primary market of the proposed course (in alphabetical order):

- Building inspectors
- Cultural heritage managers
- Federal/State disaster and emergency managers
- Fire officials
- Historical architects
- Insurance assessors
- Local government officials
- Local preservation staff
- Park Service preservation specialists
- Park Service superintendents
- Park Service wild fire/bush fire managers
- State Historic Preservation Office (SHPO) staff
- Structural engineers
- Town planners

The course is not intended to replace the skills and long experience of professionals, such as building code inspectors or historic architects, but shall provide a conceptual framework in which these professionals should operate and, most importantly, cooperate.

The undergraduate market

In addition, the standalone course can form a single unit or subject in an undergraduate course. It is projected that the subject be offered not only at Charles Sturt University, but also by a partner in the United States.

If the course is offered (predominantly) as an undergraduate subject in, say, Spring and offered as a (predominantly) professional course in Autumn, the subject can be offered all year round, giving additional flexibility to professionals and undergraduates alike.

It is anticipated that the subject can, if properly marketed, form a viable alternative as an elective subject in those degrees which allow flexibility in their structure.

Course structure and content

The course is scheduled to take six months to complete at a 0.25 study load. The educational structure underpinning the course (see below) espouses a learner-centered, problem-centered, resource-based learning environment. This allows students to progress *at their* own determined speed through the learning materials provided. While the 0.25 study load is the scheduled rate of progress, faster rates of progress are likely to become the norm.

The entire structure of the course has been designed on a fully modular basis, so that individual modules can be developed to cater for the specific needs of an audience without the need to re-write the whole subject package. For example, the subject needs to be of use both to the professional disaster manager *and* to the cultural heritage professional. The structure as envisaged would comprise of the following nine sequential modules, of which a student would need to study seven:

1. Module DIS/1: Introduction

2. Module DIS/2: What are Cultural Heritage Resources?

3. Module DIS/3: What are Natural Disasters?

4. Module DIS/4: The legal dimensions

5. Module DIS/5: Vulnerability of cultural heritage to natural disasters

6. Module DIS/6: Case studies - Geohazards

7. Module DIS/7: Case studies - Climatological hazards

8. Module DIS/8: Case studies--Human-induced hazards

9. Module DIS/9: Planning for Disasters

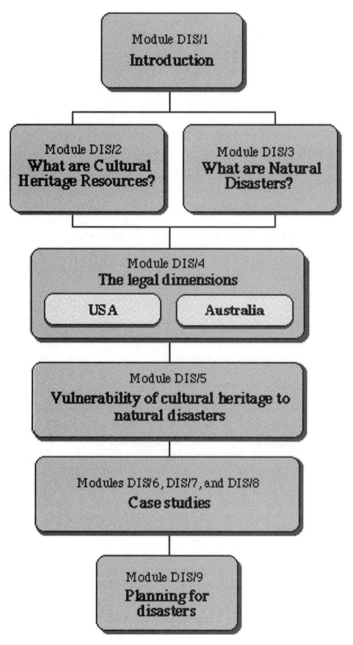

Figure 22.1. Structure of the course 'Natural Disaster Mitigation and Cultural Heritage'

Regardless from which background the prospective student or trainee comes from, he or she will start off with Module one, which sets the scene, and then choose either Module 2 or Module 3, depending on what specific knowledge is required. The student will be asked to answer an electronically marked pre-test to assess his and her knowledge level. Both streams will complete Module 4 and Module 5. Students will then choose two of Modules

6 (geohazards), 7 (climatological hazards) and 8 (human-induced hazards). Each of these modules has further options from which the students can choose. All students will then complete a disaster management plan in module 9.

Module DIS/1: Introduction

The introductory module will set the scene and provide a 'road map' for the student to provide him or her with an orientation before delving into the detailed subject matter. Also, it will include a series of self-assessments and electronically marked-up tests to allow the student to determine the level of pre-existing knowledge.

The objectives are to establish, by means of a few case examples, the potential for conflict between natural disaster managers and cultural heritage managers, and the need to find common ground on which communication can occur.

Module DIS/2: What are Cultural Heritage Resources?

This module is targeted at the natural disaster managers and the planners who are less familiar with the nature and objectives of cultural heritage management. The module will address the nature of cultural resources and will cover the concepts of cultural heritage management, from the identification and documentation of the resources to their evaluation and eventual listing. The module will include discussions on archaeological sites, the built environment as well as items of material culture and will address the issue of the variability of values and the matter of the scarcity and unrenewabality of these resources.

Module DIS/3: What are natural disasters?

This module targets the cultural heritage managers and familiarizes them with the nature of natural hazards and the objectives of natural disaster managers before, during and after a disaster event. This module will deal with geohazards and technological hazards, their nature, frequency and general impact on the environment. Each type of hazard will addressed comprehensively but succinctly. An in-depth treatment of the individual hazards and their impacts on cultural resources will occur in Module 6. Module 3 shall provide the student with a comprehensive understanding of the physical and meteorological parameters causing and governing geohazards, and shall address the concept of risk management.

Module DIS/4: The legal dimensions

This module should address issues such as the legal and administrative parameters governing the cultural heritage management agencies on the one hand, and the disaster management agencies on the other. It is this module which needs to be country-specific, as the legislation and the interpretation of these laws differs. Necessary is an overview on:

- the legislative mandate of the federal & state Emergency Management Authorities;
- the organizational/divisional structure of the federal & state Emergency Management Authorities;
- the mission(s) of the federal & state Emergency Management Authorities regarding cultural heritage;
- the policies of the federal & state Emergency Management Authorities regarding cultural heritage;

- the procedures and guidelines of the Emergency Management Authorities regarding cultural heritage;

- the legislative mandate of the federal & state Heritage Management Authorities;

- the organizational/divisional structure of the federal & state Heritage Management Authorities;

- the mission(s) of the federal & state Heritage Management Authorities regarding natural disasters;

- the policies of the federal & state Heritage Management Authorities regarding natural disasters.

In the case of the US module (Module 4 [US]), this would be *inter alia*:

- the structure of the Stafford Act;

- the mandate of FEMA;

- the structure FEMA uses to comply with its mandate;

- the mandate of State Emergency Management Authorities;

- the structure State Emergency Management Authorities use to comply with their mandate;

- the structure of the Historic Preservation Act;

- the mandate of the National Park Service;

- the administrative structure of the NPS and the SHPO's use to comply with their mandate;

- Secretary of the Interior's Standards for Rehabilitation of historic structures;

- the structure of the local heritage management agencies.

In the case of the Australian module (Module 4 [Aust]), this would be *inter alia*:

- the structure of the National Disaster Act;

- the mandate of the various state Emergency Services;

- the structure the SES use to comply with their mandate;

- the structure of the Australian Heritage Commission Act;

- the structure and mandate of the various state heritage acts;

- the structure and mandate of the local heritage management agencies.

Module DIS/5: Vulnerability of cultural heritage to natural disaster impacts

This module will address issues such as the *performance of various types* of cultural heritage (historic sites, landscapes, archaeological surface and sub-surface sites, rock art etc.), various constituent materials (wood, stone, brick, soil/adobe, textiles etc.) and structural systems (unreinforced masonry buildings, wattle-and-daub buildings, steel frame buildings etc.) in the face of the different disaster scenarios.

The common *impacts of disasters* are discussed, set out by type of cultural disaster and cross-referenced by type of resource, structural system and constituent materials. The hyper-media concept allows the student to follow through either avenue of learning.

The various *treatments and proactive measures* will be addressed, as well as the *dynamics of post-disaster actions* initiated by or taken up by the disaster victims.

Common *disaster mitigation techniques* are discussed, set out by type of disaster. What are the normal priorities of emergency response? What does this mean for historic properties? What are the logistical and operational requirements of the disaster response team? What does this imply for archaeological and heritage resources?

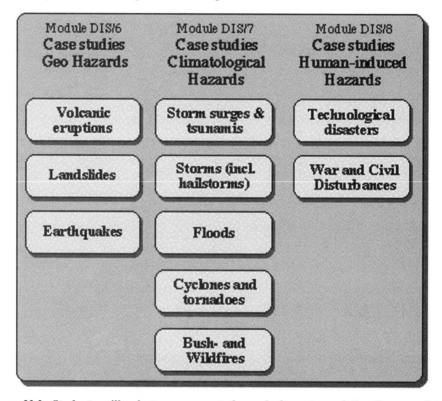

Figure 22.2. Students will select one case study each from two of the three modules.

Module DIS/6: Case Studies - Geohazards

There will be a set of modules developed for this module level, which will deal with a specific type of disaster and will address in greater detail the causes and development as well as the impact of the disaster on the cultural heritage sites. Projected are the following modules:

- Earthquakes (Module 6[a])
- Landslides (Module 6[b])
- Volcanic eruptions (Module 6[c])

Each of the case studies will make links, where appropriate, to other areas of study. For example, the effects of tsunamis are addressed in Module 7, even though they are triggered by submarine earthquakes or volcanic eruptions. It is anticipated that the sub-modules will come on line over the period of a year, starting with the most common, such as earthquakes.

Module DIS/7: Case Studies - Climatological hazards

There will be a set of modules developed for this module level, which will deal with a specific type of disaster and will address in greater detail the impact of the disaster on the cultural heritage sites. Projected are the following modules:

- Cyclones and tornadoes (Module 7[a])
- Storm surges and tsunamis (Module 7[b])
- Floods (Module 7[c])
- Storms (including hailstorms) (Module 7[d])
- Bushfires (Wildfires) (Module 7[e])

Module DIS/8: Case Studies - Human-induced hazards

There will be a set of modules developed for this module level, which will deal with a specific type of disaster and will address in greater detail the impact of the disaster on the cultural heritage sites. Projected are the following modules:

- Technological disasters (Module 8[a])
- Civil Disturbances and war (Module 8[b])

Even though the hazards included in this module are not natural disasters *sensu strictu*, many of their impacts resemble those of natural disasters. A good example is the bombing of the Murrah Federal Building in Oklahoma City, where the impact of the blast air wave had characteristics of that of cyclonic winds, and the impact of the seismic wave resembled, in part, that of earthquakes.

Module DIS/9: Planning for disasters

The final module will deal with the planning process for actions to be taken before, during and after a disaster. The student would be required to complete a disaster management plan for a specific (set of) cultural heritage place(s) and specific type of disaster, which has the greatest probability of occurring in the student's local area. This achieves a number of aims:

- it provides an assessable item for the successful completion of the subject/unit;
- it provides an applied assignment which is meaningful to the student; and
- it provides the student's employer organization with a draft disaster management plan.

The student is required to document that the plan will be workable by ensuring that appropriate communication lines have been developed, that there is stakeholder consultation on the matter and that the plan has been commented upon by at least both SHPO and the State Emergency Management Authority.

Mode of delivery

As the course is seen as a professional development option, and as hosting annual workshops is cost- and time-consuming for not only both the participants and their organizations but also for the institution hosting them, this subject package shall be delivered in external teaching mode (distance education) only. This will allow the student to complete the course at his or her own work/residential location and at the student's pace and leisure. Traditional distance education packages consist of a mail-out of course material, comprising subject outline, course/study notes and readings, often accompanied by a video tape. The set-backs of this 'traditional' mode of delivery for the purposes of this particular course subject are that, for reasons of cost, the visual images need to be kept to a few, and, for the most part, to black and white pictures.

The recent developments of server-based technology have seen the Internet become more and more pervasive. The 'information superhighway' has been touted far and wide as heralding a new age. Certainly the World Wide Web (WWW) offers a wide range of options for communication and for the exchange of information. Both individual pages of information and information exchange networks have been developed. As a result, it has become feasible to develop the course as an interactive multi-media program for delivery on the Internet/WWW which can be run 'live', downloaded to the user's PC or packaged on a CD-ROM. This approach allows for an abundance of color illustrations *and*, as well as live digital video footage to be included in the package, which can be accessed and manipulated interactively.

Charles Sturt University, as well as the author himself, has experience in developing such applications for distance education purposes (Spennemann 1995a, 1995b; Spennemann & Steinke 1995). To document the commitment to the electronic mode of delivery, this proposal has been written in Hyper Text Markup Language (HTML) and is posted on the World Wide Web at the following URL:

http://life.csu.edu.au/disaster/conf95/SFO_Course.html

The course delivery would tie in with the resources made available by and accessible through the proposed Special Interest Network on Natural Hazard Mitigation for Cultural Heritage Sites (Spennemann & Green this volume).

Educational underpinnings

The key principle of computer-driven interactive multimedia education systems is that the student is enabled to determine his or her own rate of progress through the subject matter and to conduct the self-training at self-determined intervals. With the inclusion of pictorial and audio material and the provision of multiple pathways or links, the student can effectively steer and navigate a route which will favor that particular student's mode of learning.

In general, the packages can be grouped into four classes (see below). There is a need for all four types of resources, depending on the particular learning outcome required, and none of these are the 'be-all-and-end-all' of computerized training.

Table 22.2. Classes of computer-assisted learning packages

Class	Type	Aim
I	'drill and practice'	mastery of methods/practices
II	'encyclopedia'	information resources for factual knowledge
III	'challenger'	imparting concepts and theory, thus challenging students
IV	'simulation'	application of methods, theory and factual knowledge

Multimedia *per se* do not result in increased learning and do not advance a student's understanding of the subject matter. Rather, the interactive mode of learning is the critical factor involved, as it allows the student to follow up various pathways influencing the individual learning outcome (Clark & Craig 1992).

The traditional university teaching concept entails a situation where the lecturer is in control of the information and the learning process in form of lectures and tutorials. An analysis of teaching a cultural heritage subject in an applied science context has shown that a student's migration from surface learning to deep learning is inhibited by a number of parameters, which need to be addressed systematically if the outcomes for the students shall improve:

- comfort thresholds of students to tackle challenging concepts;

- students' ability and preparedness to peruse library resources beyond the immediate need for the completion of assignment (Spennemann 1995c).

For the student's learning process, we would have to consider the following sequence:

Step 1)	Reception of ideas/information
Step 2)	Reformation of ideas integrating own experience
Step 3)	Exemplification of ideas integrating own experience
Step 4)	Generalizations from ideas
Step 5)	Generation of queries derived from ideas
Step 6)	Connections of ideas with the discourse

There is considerable literature on the cognitive parameters in relation to collaborative and problem-oriented learning and its embedding into a technological delivery framework (Soloway *et al.* 1995; Spitulnik *et al.* 1995), which shall not be reviewed here in any great detail.

The design of such packages must be centered on the learner and not the teacher (Soloway *et al.* 1995). Much of the multimedia design, such as self-guided text cum audio and still photo or text *cum* video combinations have been pre-packaged lectures and thus remain a teacher-centered design. We need to be careful not to confuse multimedia, which *sensu strictu* only means the combination of various media in one teaching package, with interactive multimedia, and interactive multimedia packages, where the student is prompted with an array of options and where the student decides the direction the inquiry shall take. On the other hand, fully learner-centered design is project- or problem-based and allows a student to solve a given problem by drawing on a variety of resources and conducting simulated experiments. Resource-based learning implies that the student is offered the resources embedded in a navigational structure which facilitate progress.

Mode and extent of assessment

At various points in each module, the student will be asked to complete in-text (in-program) activities and self-assessments tasks, as well as knowledge reaffirmation exercises. These will comprise brief evaluations or multiple choice tests contained in forms submittable on the WWW. Once a test is posted, it will be automatically marked-up by the server and once graded will be returned to the student. At the end of each module, the student will complete another multiple choice test which, once posted, will be automatically marked-up by the server *and graded*. The results contribute to the students'/participants' final grade for the subject.

The student will be required to submit only one assessable written item, a disaster management plan (see Module DIS/9), for proof of subject completion. Submission of these items can either be by ordinary mail or, preferably, in electronic form as an e-mail attachment.

On-line tutorials

One-to-one discussion and tutoring can occur via e-mail exchanges, and as a group in a virtual tutorial setting. The main aim of a newsgroup is to encourage discussion among students. Newsgroups are a unique means to blur the distinction between on-campus and distance education students, as a virtual tutorial can be established in which exchange of information can take place, inclusive of students that may otherwise not participate. If the newsgroups are structured in a fashion that ex-students are required to participate, a dynamic can be developed which draws on a wide range of expertise in the field.

Practicalities

The following practicalities need to be considered: (i) teaching responsibilities and (ii) the accreditation of the subject as a professionally recognized standalone training course.

Teaching responsibilities

The teaching and marking responsibilities should be shared between the institutions offering the course and its modules. It is envisaged that such a course would be administered as a subject by one institution (such as Charles Sturt University) and cross-listed by at least one, preferably several, US distance education providers. It is anticipated that such a course will become available by July 1996 and will be listed as a formal subject of Charles Sturt University as part of the Bachelor of Applied Science (Parks, Recreation and Heritage)[1] by January 1998 and the Bachelor of Social Science (Emergency Management)[2] by January 1998.

Accreditation

The course should be listed by one or more universities as a full subject in their degrees relating to cultural resource management, historic preservation or disaster management, which would allow a student to accrue credit towards a degree. As the subject matter has not been dealt with before in any depth, there is a need to have this subject fully accredited as a professional training and development course. In addition to accreditation through the relevant university bodies, it is suggested to register it inter alia through the following:

- American Association of Preservation Technology
- American Institute of Architects
- American Institute of Conservation Architects
- Australian Heritage Commission
- Australia ICOMOS
- Australian Archaeological Association
- Australian Emergency Management Institute
- Australian Society of Historical Archaeology
- Department of Conservation and Natural Resources (Victoria, Australia)
- Department of Environment and Heritage (Qld, Australia)
- Federal Emergency Management Agency (US)
- National Park and Wildlife Service (NSW, Australia)
- National Trust for Historic Preservation (US)
- National Trust of Australia
- US National Park Service
- USA ICOMOS

A viable option?

I believe such a course *is* a viable option. What we need to achieve is a general proprietary sense among everyone involved, that it may not be our individual property we are dealing with, but that it is *our* past, *our* heritage, a heritage which we hold in communal patrimony for *our* children - and therefore it is *our* business to look after it.

---

[1] For further information regarding this degree, contact the Administrative Officer, The School of Environmental and Information Sciences, Charles Sturt University, PO Box 789, Albury, NSW 2640, Australia.
[2] For further information regarding this degree, contact the Faculty Executive Officer, Faculty of Health, Charles Sturt University, PO Box 588, Wagga Wagga, NSW 2670, Australia.

Acknowledgments

This paper has greatly benefited from various discussions during the conference. I am particularly indebted to David W. Look and E. Blaine Cliver.

References

Blanchard, B. Wayne (1995) *Colleges, universities, and institutions offering emergency management courses*, A compilation of resources published by the Natural Hazards Center, University of Colorado at Boulder. URL: http://adder.colorado.edu/~hazctr/colleges.html

Clark, R. & Craig, T. (1992) 'Research and theory on multi-media learning effects', in *Interactive learning environments: human factors and technical considerations on design issues*, ed. M. Giardina, Springer, Berlin.

Henry, Margaret (1991) 'The battle for Newcastle: heritage and the earthquake', in *Packaging the Past? Public Histories*, eds J. Rickard & P. Spearitt, Melbourne University Press, Melbourne, pp. 102-116.

Nelson, Carl L. (1991) *Protecting the Past from Natural Disasters*, National Trust for Historic Preservation, The Preservation Press, Washington, DC.

Soloway, E., Jackson, S. L., Klein, J., Quintana, C., Reed, J., Spitulnik, J., Stratford, S. J. & Studer, S. (1995) 'Learning Theory in Practice: Case Studies of Learner-Centered Design', Technical Report, Highly Interactive Computing Group, University of Michigan, Ann Arbor, MI. URL: http://www.umich.edu/~spit/Hi-C/DIS.html

Spennemann, Dirk H. R. (1995a) 'On-line study packages for distance education. Some considerations of conceptual parameters', *Occasional Papers in Distance Education*, Open Learning Institute, Charles Sturt University, Wagga Wagga.

Spennemann, Dirk H. R. (1995b) 'Cultural Resource Management' (PKM 266), Undergraduate Subject. URL: http://life.csu.edu.au/~dspennem/PKM_266/PKM_266.html

Spennemann, Dirk H. R. (1995c) 'Skimming the bright surface, or sounding the murky depths? Teaching to learn and learning to teach Cultural Resource Management face-to-face and at a distance', in *Considering University Teaching*, Papers of the 1994 Charles Sturt University Tertiary Teaching Colloquium, eds J. Parker & R. J. Meyenn, Charles Sturt University, Bathurst, NSW.

Spennemann, Dirk H. R. & David G. Green (1995) 'A special interest network for natural hazard mitigation for cultural heritage sites', Presented to *Management of disaster mitigation and response programs for historic sites: a dialogue. San Francisco, CA, June 27-29, 1995*,
URL: SFO_SIN_Proposal.html

Spennemann, Dirk H. R. & Anthony P. Steinke (1995) 'Computerised Interactive Cultural Resources Inventory Training. A computer program for survey training at Charles Sturt University', *Johnstone Centre Report No. 32*, The Johnstone Centre, Charles Sturt University, Albury, NSW.

Spitulnik, J., Studer, S., Finkel, E., Gustafson, E., Laczko, J. & Soloway, E. (1995) 'Toward Supporting Learners. Participating in Scientifically-Informed Community Discourse', Technical Report, Highly Interactive Computing Group, University of Michigan, Ann Arbor, MI. URL: http://www.engin.umich.edu/~sstuder/CSCL.HTML

24

A special interest network for natural hazard mitigation for cultural heritage sites

DIRK H. R. SPENNEMANN & DAVID G. GREEN [¶]

This paper proposes the establishment of a Special Interest Network (SIN) on Natural Hazard Mitigation for Cultural Heritage Sites designed to provide a platform for the storage and dissemination of information on the special needs of cultural heritage sites in case of disasters. The network will provide a venue for information exchange between disaster mitigation agencies on the one hand and the cultural heritage managers on the other.

It has been asserted many times over by speakers at the symposium that there is an urgent need for the ongoing exchange of information and for a repository of relevant data. We believe that the proposed Special Interest Network will satisfy that need. This paper is based on various discussions held in San Francisco and provides a structured approach to initiate and stimulate discussion on future transnational cooperation and information exchange. The occurrence of disasters ignores state and international boundaries, and the magnitude of most disasters stretches resources beyond limits of self-reliance.

Responsible management is based on informed decisions - the better the information available, the better the decisions are likely to be. To achieve this, the relevant managers commonly draw on three sources:

1. well-structured training;

2. readily accessible information; and

3. personal or team experience.

[¶] The Johnstone Centre, Charles Sturt University, PO Box 789, Albury NSW 2640, Australia

The first can be achieved by a specialized training course at the tertiary level, either as a subject in a heritage management or disaster management degree or as a standalone professional development course. A concept for such a subject/course has been presented in a separate paper (Spennemann 1995). The level of personal or group/team experience cannot be substituted, but can be augmented by the experience of others in similar situations.

The need for up-to-date information on management options, conservation treatments, case studies and the like cannot be satisfied in a rush by traditional means once a disaster has struck. However, it can be satisfied if an information network has been established which serves all involved and which is fed by a wide range of contributors.

The target audience

The 'target audience' for the proposed special interest network consists of disaster management professionals and cultural heritage managers. In particular, this group includes (in alphabetical order):

- Building inspectors

- Cultural heritage managers

- Federal/state disaster and emergency managers

- Fire officials

- Historical architects

- Local government officials

- Local preservation staff

- Park Service preservation specialists

- Park Service superintendents

- Park Service wild fire/bush fire managers

- State Historic Preservation Office (SHPO) staff

- Structural engineers

- Town planners

The proposed SIN is not intended to replace the skills of professionals, such as building code inspectors or historic architects. On the contrary, it is intended to provide a conceptual framework within which these professionals can share their experiences and access a vast amount of relevant information.

The structure of a Special Interest Network

Perhaps the greatest immediate impact of the World Wide Web (WWW) is that it has made network publishing a viable enterprise. The advantages include instant, world-wide availability, hypertext and multimedia content and extreme flexibility in the content and format of publications. Besides traditional books and articles for instance, we can now publish data, software, images, animation and audio.

There is a growing trend in many areas of research towards large-scale projects and studies that involve contributions from many sources (Green 1993). Also, there is no need for a 'publication' to be stored all in one place. For instance, acting independently, many Web sites have put together national or regional guides. Many of these documents, such as the *Guide to Australia* integrate information from many different sources.   In turn, these documents are now themselves being merged to form encyclopedic information bases, such as the *Virtual Tourist*.

There are also great advantages in publishing raw data, as well as the conclusions of scientific studies. In many cases, data that are gathered for one purpose can be 'recycled' and, combined with other data, add value to related studies.

A SIN is a group of people and/or institutions who collaborate to provide information about a particular subject. The main functions of a SIN fall into the following four headings:

    1. Publication

       The SIN publishes information on the specialist topic. Besides articles and books in the traditional sense, publications can also include datasets, images, audio and software. SINs adopt the fundamental principle that the supplier of a piece of information is also the publisher; that is, rather than take (say) data from many different sites and place it all on a single server, each site runs its own server and publishes its own data. The logical endpoint of this trend would be a server *on every* computer, with every individual user being his/her own publisher!

    2. Virtual Library

       The SIN provides users with access to information on the specialist topic. Besides information stored on-site, there are links to relevant information elsewhere.

    3. On-line Services

       The SIN might provide relevant services, such as analyzing data, to its users.

    4. Communications

       The SIN provides a means for people in the field to keep in touch. This might include mailing lists, newsgroups, newsletters and conferences.

SINs consist of a series of participating 'nodes' that each contribute to the network's functions. More specifically, the nodes carry one or more of the following:

- Accept and store relevant, contributed material;

- Provide some form of public access for users;

- Provide some unique information, or mirror other sites;

- Provide organized links to other nodes;

- Coordinate their activity with other nodes.

For research activity, SINs are the modern equivalent of learned societies. Some may even be the communications medium for societies (for example, Burdet 1992). We can also consider SINs as a logical extension of newsgroups and bulletin boards; namely, they aim to provide a complete working environment for their members and users. SINs differ from special interest groups (SIGs) in two important ways. Firstly, SIGs are usually part of larger organizations. The second, and greater, distinction lies in the use of networks. Whereas a group usually has a focus, SINs are explicitly decentralized.

A good example of a SIN is the European Molecular Biology Network. EMBNet is a special interest network that serves the European molecular biology and biotechnology research community. It consists of nodes operated by biologically oriented centers   in different European countries. It features a number of services and activities, especially genomic databases such as EMBL (Cameron 1988).

The following features characterize most large special interest networks. They also provide guidelines for setting one up.

Need

The SIN serves a need that is not being met by other means, or provides a better (more comprehensive, accurate or reliable) set of data than is available from other sources.

Coordination

A coordinating center or syndicate organizes the network, receives and processes new entries and communicates relevant news to its users.

Support

There is a body of users who are willing and able to help to establish and manage the network's information activities (managing databases, editing publications, moderating newsgroups, mailing lists, etc.).

Participation

Anyone may contribute items to the information base. Major SINs announce new entries via special newsgroups or mailing lists. Contributors carry out all editing of their entries, including formatting, correcting and updating them.

Access

Anyone may access, copy or use the information at any time. Normally access is via a computing network using a standard protocol.

Standards

Contributors must use standard fields and attributes in submissions (for example Croft, 1989). These standards must be well defined and should be publicized as widely as possible. For data, they are often expressed as a submission form (electronic, printed, or both) that is filled in by contributors (see later).

Format

Textual data (including bibliographies, mailing lists, etc.) are normally submitted as ASCII files with embedded tags. The Standard Generalized Markup Language (SGML) provides a flexible medium for 'marking up' information for a variety of purposes. The Hypertext Markup Language (HTML), which is an SGML application, is used for formatting documents for distribution via the WWW. However, there are many advantages in marking up documents using structural tags, rather than HTML's predominantly formatting tags. This practice allows great flexibility in the way servers access information. For instance, equivalent sections (for example, bibliographies) can be automatically extracted from many different files, combined, reformatted and delivered as a Web document. On any particular node, databases can be stored using any database software, provided that a suitable network gateway can be provided. Utilities for SQL/HTML conversion are now widely available, for instance. Images should be in one of the common formats in use, such as GIF (Graphic Interchange Format) or JPEG (Joint Photographic Experts Group).

Quality control

Users need some guarantee that data provided in a database are both valid and accurate. Quality control checks can be applied by database contributors, coordinators, and users (see later).

Attribution

Every item of information should include an indication of its contributor. This is essential to the notion that contributions are a form of publication.

Agreements

There is an explicit list of terms and conditions. Typically, users agree to acknowledge the sources and to waive liability for any use they make of the data. Contributors agree to place their data in the public domain. The organizers agree to abide by the usual conditions for publications, such as referring corrections or changes to the contributors. Everyone agrees not to sell or charge for the data.

Automation

As many operations as possible (for example, logging and acknowledging submissions) should be automated (Figure 1).

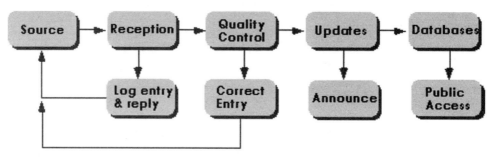

Figure 23.1.   Stages in the publication of information on a node of a SIN.   As many steps as possible should be automated.

Further and more detailed information on Special Interest Networks can be found in Green 1994.

Nodes

At present, it is suggested that nodes be established in each of the major global areas; that is, in the Americas, Australasia/Oceania and Europe/Africa.

The Americas

Given the involvement of the US National Park Service, and the development of the Historic Preservation Training Center at Natchitoches, Louisiana in the management of disaster mitigation measures, it would be appropriate to locate one node at this facility. The commitment of the Federal Emergency Management Agency (FEMA) to the preservation of cultural heritage in the face of natural disasters may necessitate the establishment of another node at FEMA in Washington, DC.

Australasia/Oceania

Charles Sturt University (http://www.csu.edu.au/) is implementing SINs to support a wide range of interests, especially in education and research. The University has established a disaster management course and has an active research interest in the implication of natural hazards on cultural as well as environmental resources through The Johnstone Centre.

Europe/Africa

To be decided.

Management responsibilities

An information system that is distributed over several sites   (nodes) requires close coordination between the sites involved. The coordinators need to agree on the following points:

- logical structure of the on-line information;

- separation of function between the sites involved;

- attribute standards for submissions (see below);

- protocols for submission of entries, corrections, etc.;

- quality control criteria and procedures (see below);

- protocols for on-line searching of the databases;

- protocols for 'mirroring' the data sets.

For instance, an international natural hazard mitigation database project might consist of agreements on the above points by a set or participating sites ('nodes'). Contributors could submit their entries to any node and each node would either 'mirror' the others or else provide on-line links to them.

A viable option?

We believe that the development of a such a SIN is a viable option. Moreover, we believe the time is right for such a network to be established. The San Francisco conference has shown that the various parties are interested in increased communication and cooperation. A special interest network is the right vehicle to achieve this aim.

Examples of SINS

Many organizations are adopting the *de facto* SINs approach as suggested here. For example:

- The Biodiversity Information Network (BIN21),
  which is located at http://www.ftpt.br/bin21/bin21.html

- FireNet, with CSU's node at http://www.csu.edu.au/firenet/

- Charles Sturt University (http://www.csu.edu.au/) is implementing SINs to support a wide range of interests, especially in education and research.

References

Burdet, H. M. (1992) 'What is IOPI?', *Taxon*, 41: 390-392.

Cameron, G. N. (1988) 'The EMBL data library', *Nucl. Acids Res.*, 16: 1865-1867.

Croft, J. R.   (1989) *Herbarium information standards and protocols for interchange of data*, Australian National Botanic Gardens, Canberra.

Green, D. G. (1993) 'Databasing the world', *INQUA - Commission for the Study of the Holocene, Working Group on Data-Handling Methods*, 9: 12-17.
URL. http://life.anu.edu.au/landscape_ecology/inqua.html

Green, D. G. (1994) 'A Web of SINs - the nature and organization of Special Interest Networks'.
URL http://www.csu.edu.au/links/sin/sin.html

Spennemann, Dirk H. R. (1995) 'Natural Disaster Mitigation and Cultural Heritage: a course proposal', Paper presented to *Management of disaster mitigation and response programs for historic sites: a dialogue*, San Francisco, CA, June 27-29.
URL. http://life.csu.edu.au/disaster/conf95/SFO_Course.html

THE FUTURE

Spennemann, Dirk H. R. & David W. Look (1998)
'From conflict to dialogue, from dialogue to cooperation,
from cooperation to preservation', in *Disaster
Management Programs for Historic Sites*, eds Dirk H. R.
Spennemann & David W. Look. San Francisco and
Albury: Association for Preservation Technology
(Western Chapter) and The Johnstone Centre, Charles
Sturt University. Pp. 175-188.

25

From conflict to dialogue, from dialogue to cooperation, from cooperation to preservation

DIRK H. R. SPENNEMANN [¶]
DAVID W. LOOK [†]

Symposia like this on the Management of Disaster Mitigation Programs for Historic Sites are very useful indeed as they open up channels of communication on both a formal and informal level. We believe that the San Francisco symposium has been a successful voyage across a treacherous sea: interagency rivalry, misunderstanding, territorial demarcation, sheer ignorance of others' concerns and a whole lot more. Some of this was implied, some covertly expressed. On occasion, some was institutional 'baggage' shining through. A feeling of unequal relationship between the players in the game was expressed. All of this is human.

However, by allowing each other to see the other side it should have become clear that not all is dark over there and that not all is light over here either. Disasters do not discriminate how they affect culturally significant and culturally insignificant resources, but we, as managers of these cultural resources, or we, as managers of the mitigation efforts, can.

Whilst the following represents a summary of what we deem to be the significant, real and positive outcomes of this symposium and the areas where we feel some more effort and goodwill needs to be expended, we are not so arrogant to claim "Hey, have *we* got a solution for you!".

[¶] The Johnstone Centre, Charles Sturt University, PO Box 789, Albury NSW 2640, Australia.
E-mail: dspennemann@csu.edu.au
[†] US National Park Service, Western Regional Office, 600 Harrison Street, San Francisco, CA 94104-1372, USA.
E-mail: david_w._look@nps.gov

From conflict to dialogue

The need for (more) understanding

There was clearly a need to explain to each other what one's own agency actually did on the federal level, the state level *and* the local government level. Both major players, the US National Park Service and the Federal Emergency Management Agency (FEMA), have to continue to explain their legal authorities and requirements, as well as the procedures adopted and the management philosophy espoused. As the logo for the Symposium shows, the responsibilities of FEMA and National Park Service only overlap when cultural resources are effected by disaster mitigation and response.

Most of the negative experiences of past disaster response periods seem to have arisen from what is frequently incorrectly perceived as interagency rivalry and mistrust exacerbated by a lack of understanding and communication (Katchka this volume). In part this is due to the different institutional missions and priorities into which new members (staff) are oriented, focused and trained. As Kimmelman (this volume) warns, differences in institutional culture cannot be understated. Yet we believe these are unnecessary constraints which must be overcome. Communication is a key to successful cooperation. However, communication must not be limited to 'umbrella' agreements between the heads of the agencies; it must filter down and be established at all levels of the administrative hierarchy, both at a formal and at an informal level.

Figure 24.1. Interagency collaboration in action. Staff of the Georgia State Historic Preservation Office, the National Trust and the Federal Emergency Management Agency consult with Georgia department of Natural Resources law enforcement officers during an assessment of the flood damage following the flooding by Tropical Storm Alberto. (Photo: Jim Lockhart 1994).

In addition to differences in the specific languages/terminologies used by the agencies, a common issue is the differences in perception of the other agencies' priorities. On the one hand, historic preservationists often believe emergency management agencies to be oblivious to the heritage values of a place while, on the other hand, disaster management agencies often assume that the cultural heritage professionals wished to protect *everything* and that there was no prioritization of sites. The development of a threat matrix model for sites affected, or potentially affected, by the Exxon Valdez oil spill (Kurtz 1995) was a good example how to overcome such misunderstandings.

'The color of money'

Shortly after a disaster occurs, economic considerations come into play. Is it economical to rehabilitate a historic structure? Who pays for the demolition of a structure if one waits beyond the 30-day grace period provided by FEMA?

What is the color of money during a disaster? It is not green; it is red. Just as we are dealing with red-tagged buildings, we are dealing with pennies when we discuss the value of heritage buildings. Bright red (-tagged?) pennies, being counted - somewhere. We are not arguing against budget constraint, or against 'cost beneficial aspects' - to use that beautiful euphemism for cost effectiveness. What we would like to question is the *way* they are counted.

Damaged buildings are tagged based on a preliminary inspection, usually twenty minutes or less. There is a general misunderstanding by the public caused by a misconception in the mass media that all red-tagged buildings must be demolished. The truth is that the red tag only means that the building is considered unsafe to enter at this time and needs further investigation. This may lead to stabilization and repair or it may lead to demolition if the owner is unable or unwilling to pay for the needed work. There are few historic buildings that cannot be stabilized, repaired, retrofitted and reconstructed as witnessed by other cultures around the world.

Buildings can be assessed by the real estate market values, and this concept can be applied to the actual costs incurred during seismic retrofit and the like. Even the economic guidelines given to owners of heritage properties are biased towards demolition and replacement with new buildings. The California State Building Seismic Program, for example, recommends the replacement of a historic structure if the cost of retrofitting an existing building exceeds 120% of the cost of a new building (Donaldson this volume). While this compares favorably with the 60% ratio recommended for non-heritage buildings, these figures, even if based on accurate estimates of the retrofit costs, do not consider values other than those covered by real estate.

Can we apply pure market values to an entity which has intrinsic values - intrinsic values which are based on social constructs of significance and importance? Would it not be prudent to conduct contingent valuation exercises to look at the non-market economics hidden in the picture? These non-market, or amenity values, may well skyrocket the 'value' of many sites. We need to look at this aspect before we jump to conclusions and make far-ranging decisions.

Consequently, Mackensen (this volume) argues for a sliding scale of cost multipliers before demolition becomes an option. He likens this level of protection to that of home insurance where insurance does not cover the depreciated value of the goods or the value of new goods, but the replacement value of the goods damaged.

Retribution

Disasters exert trauma among the victims and there is an inescapable urge to seek retribution, to vent anger and to seek vengeance. As there are no guilty parties that can be condemned easily, the initial anger is vented against the rem(a)inders of the event: the damaged structures. As Widell (this volume) put it: "In time of emergency, when our human instinct is crying to gain control, to strike back and show strength, demolition nicely fills those needs".

As Kariotis (this volume) points out, we have developed strange views about what is hazardous. The risk posed by earthquake-damaged buildings pales in comparison to the risk posed by traffic accidents. But as David Look said "After a car accident no-one shoots the car. So why do we demolish historic buildings after an earthquake?". Indeed, why do we?

Figure 24.2. A case of retribution. The Oddfellows Fraternal Hall, Watsonville, CA, was damaged during the 1989 Loma Prieta earthquake, the falling parapet masonry killing a pedestrian. Although repairable, the building was quickly demolished a few days after the disaster. The tower is a wood frame construction with metal covering and did not fail during the earthquake event. (Photo: Steade Craigo 1989).

There are two major agendas being played out in the demolition of heritage buildings. People are concerned, rightly or wrongly, that the buildings pose an inherent danger to the public, that they are beyond repair and that they should be demolished as a public safety measure; and then there are those who take advantage of the disaster situation to rid themselves of heritage-listed structures deemed to be 'standing in the way' of urban redevelopment. The result of both is the same: properties either on heritage registers or eligible for inclusion are demolished.

Even though California, for example, stipulates that State Historical Preservation Office (SHPO) approval is required for demolition, even in emergency situations, a 'rider' still exists which permits demolition without approval if an imminent threat to life safety or the adjacent buildings exists (Craigo this volume). This provision can be, and has been, interpreted with substantial latitude, especially as this determination is made at the local level Donaldson this volume).

Clearly there is a need for the public to appreciate that solutions other than demolition exist and can be used. As Craigo (this volume) points out, many owners were not willing or able to challenge demolition orders. The acquiescence to demolition was also reinforced by the fact that the demolition costs would be borne by the federal government for a period of thirty days following a disaster. Often what people were not told was that FEMA would also pay for shoring up, stabilization and fencing of damaged structures (Craigo this volume). Federal funds, however, are not available to pay for the repair of structures. Following disasters, the Small Business Administration offers low-interest loans (Brantley 1995) but even these are unaffordable for some of the victims. As a result, demolition and new construction is seen as the cheaper alternative, especially as the demolition is cost-neutral to the owner or is advantageous to one who wants a cleared site in order to redevelop.

The recognition of significant historic character and fabric, archaic materials and earlier building systems and technology is an important element in conservation. While heritage management should not willfully endanger human lives in a disaster situation, the issue of acceptable risk needs to be carefully assessed. It is all too easy to assume that no risk is acceptable and that all structures need to be 'safe'.

The maintenance of older, damaged structures is often inhibited by the tendency of local government authorities to require that the repaired structure now comply will all *current* building standards imposed on new construction, even though an identical, undamaged historic structure is not required to do so. As Mackensen (this volume) points out, this not only adds to the delay in conservation action, but also, and importantly, adds to the financial and emotional costs to the property owner.

Hasty demolition of 'unwanted' heritage-listed structures is not uncommon. Camouflaged as a public safety measure, property owners call in work teams to demolish red-tagged structures before authorities can act.

This is on record for several localities in California following Loma Prieta (Craigo this volume) as well as following the Newcastle Earthquake of 1989 in Australia. The most blatant example in Newcastle was the demolition of the Century Theater where the damage was restricted to a collapsed awning, yet the building was demolished (Henry 1991).

From dialogue to cooperation

The need for standardization

While the National Historic Preservation Act applies uniformly across the United States, and while National Historic Preservation Act, Section 106, approval requirements are also national, each individual state has its own variation of a historic preservation act with different administrative requirements and stipulations. State emergency agencies are aware of these needs and administrative structures. Yet during natural disasters, emergency management commonly also draws on federal agencies, and it is here where problems arise.

Federal agencies, such as FEMA, which are responsible for regions encompassing several states, need to be able to respond to the primary objectives of disaster management to save lives and property in quickly and comprehensively.

Clearly, the variations in state requirement with respect to historic preservation are not conducive to rapid responses. The Midwest Floods of 1993 are an example of where a single disaster affects several states and where a regionally coordinated response potentially runs foul of varied state requirements. Programmatic agreements standardizing the responses and clearly outlining the processes and responsibilities are the obvious answer. As Katchka (this volume) has shown, the key to a successful programmatic agreement is to anticipate the issues of conflict that might arise and to design resolution mechanisms. Clearly, as the programmatic agreements are being executed, lessons are learned and included in future agreements of this sort.

The need for (more) education

A common theme was the need for more public education, but just throwing information at people is no more going to help than just throwing money at the problem. The educational efforts must be focused and targeted to specific audiences; therefore they need to be i) multi-faceted and ii) custom-tailored to the clientele they shall educate (cf., Spennemann this volume).

Public education

As Craigo (this volume) pointed out, a disaster victim is simply not going to be very receptive when confronted with a smartly dressed person flatly stating "I am from the government and I am here to help you." The victim is overwhelmed by his or her experience, is most likely in a state of delayed shock and is quite understandably preoccupied with more pressing issues. Unless the disaster victim has been 'preconditioned' to the nature and extent of the help which can be expected, the help offered for the retention of a historic property may not be very welcome.

Public propaganda campaigns for the general populace are necessary, but will most likely be limited to a 'shotgun approach': widely scattered but of limited impact. Targeted, high impact public education campaigns need to focus on the owners *and* occupiers (which need not be the same) of every single property listed on the National Register or included in historic districts: a huge task, no doubt, but a necessary one, as it will also function in raising the owner's/occupier's awareness of the importance of the residence; and, if coupled with a targeted campaign to inform on maintenance issues, much goodwill can come of it.

There can be little doubt that the community is preoccupied with short-term concerns and issues rather than long-term ones. Hence, education for events that are likely to occur, yet at an unspecified and unspecifiable date will fall on deaf ears. Throughout California there is a nature, if not culture, of denial even though another strong and eminently destructive earthquake event is inevitable. No matter how much public education occurs, some members of the public will remain in denial.

Professional education

Like the disaster victim, local building inspectors or structural engineers are not likely to be receptive to the real or perceived (and thus 'real') 'intrusion' of heritage managers when they are worrying about tagging buildings and keeping the mayor and other local omni-potentiaries off their backs. Handing out information packs containing legal information and ordinances after an event as suggested by Donaldson (this volume) is all very well, but not likely to fall on receptive ears. Training must have been completed *beforehand* and at a level which makes the relevant official feel comfortable about including the knowledge gained in the decision-making process on the spot. After the event has occurred, a short intensive refresher briefing at public meetings can reinforce the training. This was very effective in Los Gatos.

Barksdale (this volume) shows that technical education before, during and after a disaster is crucial to the survival of historic places.

One of the most unnecessary side-effects of many natural disasters is the loss of highly significant aspects of a nation's cultural heritage. Insufficient knowledge of the importance and management of such places leads to well intentioned mitigation efforts which unfortunately impair or destroy cultural heritage. This can be overcome by a training course which focuses on the principles of disaster mitigation and cultural heritage management and addresses the specific mitigation needs of, and conservation options for, heritage sites. A training course should be developed and offered by distance education as a university subject and as a professional development and/or continuing education course. Such a training course would facilitate in-house and in-work training of staff and would render obsolete the currently prevailing climate of misunderstanding and non-implementation of appropriate actions and safeguards.

To sum up, the education shall increase the level of public understanding in general; the level of specific knowledge of the house owners/occupiers; and the level of skills *and understanding* of heritage matters by non-heritage disciplines, and of disaster matters by non-disaster disciplines.

Communications

In the past, some negative experiences have derived from interagency 'turf wars' and simple misunderstandings as a result of a lack of communication. But communication must not be restricted to the disaster phase alone.

Repeatedly, the need to maintain lines of communication has been stressed. As a result, taskforces on heritage needs in disaster situations have been formed (Cliver this volume). However, we should not confine this communication to top-level connections at high-level meetings. These meetings and connections are fine, but they do not translate into trust. These meetings only too often translate into decrees: *Thou shalt talk to (liaise with) the NPS / FEMA / OES / SHPO / ACHP....*Such approaches are not really conducive to building up trust, but trust is what underpins successful management. In a disaster situation, we simply do not have the time, nor the energy to work out whether some 'drop-in' from another agency is actually any good at his or her job. Consequently, he or she is given the 'arms-length treatment' rather than putting the person straight to work.

Communication must occur across the board and may well involve going across town, or - god forbid! - across the corridor and joining in at a tea or coffee hour for a chat. Socialization in others' institutional culture will pay off.

The media have been identified by several as one of the major agents of hasty change. Always hungry for gory details, non-spectacular results are not newsworthy. However, if a good relationship has developed, it should be *good* news that our stock of historic buildings has survived the earthquake well. The message is that the anchor to a past splendid is still there, thereby potentially providing emotional fix points.

Such news does not generate itself; *we* have to precondition the 'bloodhounds' of the media and *we* have to 'put a spin on it'. All of this is basic politics of image creation, well known to all of us. Let's do it!

Support

It has become clear that disasters simply over-stretch the resources and capacities of the local staff. What can be done?

Building on the FEMA concept of having a register of available professional staff which FEMA can borrow from other agencies in case of an emergency, it may well be a sensible idea to pull in a small Heritage Damage Assessment Task Force from interstate. This task force would assist the local staff in the verification of red-tag decisions, run routine section 106 matters, provide instant advice to home owners and so forth. But these are not the only benefits. Consider also that such a team would:

- fill the gap of the first two weeks before 'standard' responses 'kick in';
- experience the trauma following an actual event (rather than simply relying on theory);
- gain actual first-line people management skills;
- develop team relationships;
- work out 'snags' in the team's communication with the emergency services; and
- establish close relationships with other state teams.

If a disaster were to strike in the home town/state of the team, the team would 'hit the ground running'. No start-up period, no time wasted getting to know each others' idiosyncrasies and so forth. Responsibilities and skills are well understood, and the team is 'in business' from the first minute onwards. It would be well trained, 'battle-hardened' and would already have working relationships with the other Heritage Damage Assessment Task Forces coming in from interstate to help.

Any Heritage Damage Assessment Task Force leaving for an emergency call should not have more than 10% new (that is, untrained) people. This maintains stability thereby ensuring well oiled operations. The composition of the taskforce should include FEMA, Office of Emergency Services (or state equivalent), SHPO and National Park Service, augmented on the ground by a person from the local preservation support group or historical society to provide information on local politics and other constraints.

It is obviously a reciprocal structure which, in the climate of cost-cutting and downsizing, may sit uncomfortably with some administrators, but we believe it is a 'safety net' well worth weaving. It cannot work on its own and needs to be linked with public education programs (mentioned above) and good lines of communication. The 'nitty gritty' of the matter, of course, is to work out who 'picks up the slack' left behind at the office back home.

Cultural sensitivities

An issue mentioned by Coshigiano (1995) and, in passing, alluded to by other speakers, is the sensitivity of the disaster managers to the specific needs of cultures other than the dominant Anglo-Saxon/Anglo-European conglomerate. Non-European cultures need to be respected and, if possible, understood. The disaster response team must be culturally sensitive and understand that levels of acceptable risk are cultural constructs and differ from culture to culture, and that, by implication, the priorities for mitigation efforts will vary from group to group. While this is particularly true for members of the Native Americans, Hawaiians and Micronesians, it is applicable to other ethnic minorities as well. The United States is a multicultural society and this needs to be taken into account.

Katchka (this volume) touches upon the issue of stakeholder identification and who should be consulted in the formulation of a memorandum of agreement. Clearly, as she points out, the process has to be holistic and needs to be more compassing than merely drawing on individuals recognized by the United States as being legal descendants of tribal descent. Ultimately, broad community support and *consensus* decisions are needed if proposed agreements shall have longevity and success.

One of the issues recurrently encountered in Australian cultural resource management is the sacred sites. These do not figure on any register as they are no-one's business except that of the specific local group and their custodians. These sites are only mentioned when the sites are actually threatened. Likewise, there are men's and women's sites, and it is totally inappropriate for a man to enter a woman's site, no matter what the circumstances. In the US scenario, a good solution to the problem would be the close involvement of Native American Indian groups as full stakeholders in the development of disaster response plans, and to include one or - if gender issues are important to the local community - two representative(s) on the cultural heritage assessment task force who can provide instant advice.

From cooperation to preservation

Proactive versus reactive management

The loss of any historic fabric is deplorable as it is irreplaceable in its own right, as any loss of original fabric will reduce the historical integrity of a structure. It can be repaired but, once damage occurs, the resource is never the same again. Thus, is it not better to mitigate a hazard than to mitigate the effects of the disaster?

Seismic retrofit has been addressed many times over, but there are only a few references of retrofit and preventative mitigation for other disasters types (roofs can be better anchored for hurricanes and typhoons). Across the board we are in dire need of proactive management.

Following the Loma Prieta Earthquake, state building codes were revised (Mathison this volume) leading to greater protection, but also some undesirable effects. The California building code, for example, requires local government entities to identify potentially dangerous unreinforced masonry structures and to develop plans for mitigating hazards derived from these places. While the California Unreinforced Masonry Law does not require owners to retrofit their buildings, the local government entities, fearing liability lawsuits, adopted mandatory seismic retrofit ordinances (Craigo this volume). While these ordinances permitted, in the case of non-compliance, the demolition of the structure, the owners were not given avenues of financial assistance to retrofit.

There can be little doubt that mandatory programs of seismic retrofit, such as San Francisco's parapet abatement program and the Los Angeles unreinforced masonry abatement program, saved lives in the respective earthquake events. It is questionable though, whether non-compliance on financial grounds should lead to the loss of heritage structures. It is incumbent on the local government agencies to consider financial incentives, such as property tax rate freezes or rate rebates (which should be means-tested), to ensure the survival of historically significant neighborhoods.

The various bond proposals issued by the City and County of San Francisco, and the approval of these proposals by vote of the general public shows that there is widespread community support for the rehabilitation and seismic retrofit of public structures, even if this requires the commitment of substantial funding (Alfaro this volume).

As historic structures are a finite resource, and an assessable resource at that, it should be possible, where required, to develop individual assessments and individual disaster response methodologies for each structure well and truly before a disaster strikes (Donaldson this volume).

Blaine Cliver's tale of the mitigation of the effects of a fire at Frank Delano Roosevelt's mansion is a salient point: proactive management in the form of disaster preparedness training and a disaster plan facilitated the successful containment of the blaze (Cliver this volume). We can only hope that, in five years time, such a tale is *so* commonplace that it is no longer worth mentioning.

The advances in portable computer technology allow us to conduct structure assessments and enter the information into databases. Craigo (this volume) described how the SHPO database of historic properties could be electronically compared to the database of damaged properties as assessed by the emergency services. The filtering process identified the damaged heritage properties which could then be independently assessed. While this is an obvious solution and clearly a labor-saving advancement, this system is only as good as the historic properties database. If the database includes all properties, both on the register of historic places and those properties eligible for inclusion, then a safety net has been achieved. If, however, as is too often the case in communities not overly concerned with heritage issues, the register of historic properties is minimalist or thematically skewed, with little interest in achieving a comprehensive listing, then a database comparison will only identify the most significant properties at risk.

Barksdale (this volume) describes the scenario in Georgia following Tropical Storm Alberto. Even though register listings had been carried out, the rural areas were less well researched, surveyed and documented and, as a result, the disaster responses were hampered and organized damage assessments made difficult.

It must be clear to all involved that such a filtering process is only the first step in the assessment of historic structures, targeting those identified as significant and at risk. Yet we should not lose sight that adjoining properties, in themselves possibly not significant, contribute to the setting of the historic pace and may need to be saved as well or else the setting of the listed structure, and possibly the whole neighborhood, will suffer.

Application of the precautionary principle

Another issue raised by some of the speakers was the debate about whether a particular place or building was historically significant or not and, hence, whether any management controls should 'kick in'. Why is it important to establish *immediately after a disaster* whether a building is significant? We are aware of the 30-day period for funded demolition, but why not use the precautionary principle and, in the post disaster phase, simply *assume* the building to be significant and eligible for inclusion in the register - *until proven otherwise*?

Donaldson (this volume) argues for a regular and qualified second opinion for all decisions involving demolition and significant loss of historic fabric.

This may well mean that a rule change needs to occur and that the 30-day funded demolition period may need to be extended. But - with some goodwill - it should not be much of an administrative 'high wire act' to develop a list of buildings for which conditional demolition approval has been given, thus ensuring that the 30-day rule stays intact. The final decision on this, however, will depend on the findings of the historic preservation disaster assessment task force. If the building is really so damaged that it needs to be demolished, then a delay of another three weeks or so will not matter.

However, it may matter psychologically as the disaster victims may wish to 'draw a line' under the events and start afresh from a clean building lot, so to speak. This is an issue that can be pre-empted by adequate and ongoing public education.

Disaster planning

While earthquakes are predictable in their occurrence *per se*, but not in their magnitude and timing, other natural disasters can be predicted with reasonable accuracy a few days prior to their occurrence. This is certainly true for cyclones/hurricanes and river floods which are seasonal events. In addition, the linkages between global climatic conditions, such as El Niño, and the frequency of natural disasters has been shown. This allows public officials to predict a higher probability of disasters during some years (cf., Spennemann & Marschner 1995). Clearly, there is a need for predictive modeling and disaster planning which is based on long-term and short-term preparation.

Since cyclones/hurricanes come with a warning period, we can implement last-minute disaster preparedness activities for heritage places and conduct last-minute 'refresher' education campaigns to home-owners; also the communications lines between the various agencies can be reopened should this prove to be necessary.

The disaster planning components need, on the one hand, to clearly define the role of the historic preservation specialists, and the Programmatic Agreements and Memoranda of Agreement are a good step in this process. On the local level, there need to be plans in place which assign meaningful roles to local preservation specialists.

It should be feasible, for example, to compile a register of historic architects willing to donate some of their time *pro bono publico* after a disaster event to assess the mitigation options for damaged structures and to determine a rough estimate of the cost of these actions. This register needs to be maintained on a regular basis and the volunteers on the register need to be trained in emergency management procedures.

The road ahead

One of the major components we need to consider is training of staff at all levels of disaster management in the appropriate treatment of cultural resources. Workshops and Symposia such as the one held in San Francisco particularly targeted front line staff, not heads of agencies. These must be coordinated with department head summits so there is support from the top.

If the achievements of this symposium merely remain a new set of cooperative agreements handed down with authority by the authority, it is 'just another rule' to follow, and this would resemble a free-standing arch: two monolithic pillars connected at the top only by unbraced vossoirs (the stones on each side of the keystone) - and we know what happens to that in earthquakes. What we need to achieve is a structure where these monolithic stones are tied together by shear walls and cross-braces to form a strong unit swinging at the same wavelength.

What we need to achieve is a general proprietary sense among everyone involved; that it may not be *our* property that we are dealing with, but that it is *our* past, *our* heritage - a heritage which *we* hold in communal patrimony for *our* children. Therefore it is *our* inalienable responsibility to look after it, and to do that well.

References

Alfaro, J. (1998) 'The role of federal disaster relief assistance to local communities for historic preservation', this volume.

Barksdale, D. (1998) 'Disaster recovery response to Tropical Storm Alberto', this volume.

Brantley, B (1995) 'The loan program of the Small Business Administration and its role in the recovery following a disaster', Paper presented presented to *Management of disaster mitigation and response programs for historic sites: a dialogue. San Francisco, CA. June 27-29, 1995*, San Francisco, CA: US National Park Service, Western Regional Office and Western Chapter of the Association of Preservation Technology.

Cliver, E. Blaine (1998) 'Assessing the character and systems of historic buildings', this volume.

Craigo, S. (1998a) 'A helping hand', this volume.

Coshigiano, D-M. (1995) 'Typhoon INIKI and its aftermath', Paper presented to *Management of disaster mitigation and response programs for historic sites: a dialogue. San Francisco, CA. June 27-29, 1995*, San Francisco, CA: US National Park Service, Western Regional Office and Western Chapter of the Association of Preservation Technology.

Donaldson, W. (1998) 'The first ten days: emergency response and protection strategies for the preservation of historic structures', this volume.

Henry, M. (1991) 'The battle for Newcastle: heritage and the earthquake,' *Australian Historical Studies*, 24(96): 102-116.

Kariotis, J. (1998) 'The tendency to demolish repairable structures in the name of 'life safety'', this volume.

Katchka, L. (1998) 'Memorandum of Agreement and Programmatic Agreements in the disaster context', this volume.

Kimmelman, A. (1998) 'Cultural heritage and disaster management in Tucson, Arizona', this volume.

Kurtz, S. (1995) 'Management and Mitigation: The aftermath of the Exxon Valdez oil spill,' *Paper presented to Management of disaster mitigation and response programs for historic sites: a dialogue. San Francisco, CA. June 27-29, 1995*, San Francisco, CA: US National Park Service, Western Regional Office and Western Chapter of the Association of Preservation Technology.

Mackensen, R. (1998) 'Cultural heritage management and California's State Historical Building Code', this volume.

Mathison, S. A. (1998) 'The Secretary of the Interior's standards for rehabilitation pertinent to cultural resources affected by disasters', this volume.

Spennemann, D. H. R. (1998) 'Natural disaster mitigation and cultural heritage: a course proposal', this volume.

Spennemann, D. H. R. & Marschner, I. (1995) 'Association between ENSO and typhoons in the Marshall Islands,' *Disasters*, 19(3): 194-197.

Widell, C. (1998) 'The government's responsibilities for the preservation of private and public cultural resources at federal, state and local levels', this volume.

Contributors

Jorge Alfaro — Chief of Staff, Department of Public Works, San Francisco, California, CA 94102, USA

Alice M. Baldrica — Archaeologist, Nevada State Historic Preservation Office, Nevada State Historic Preservation Office, 100 South Stewart Street, Capitol Complex, Carson City, Nevada 89710, USA

Daryl Barksdale — Flood Assistance Coordinator, Georgia Historic Preservation Division, Department of Natural Resources, 205 Butler Street, SE, Suite 1462, Atlanta, GA 30334, USA

E. Blaine Cliver — Chief, Preservation Assistance Division, National Park Service, PO Box 37127, Washington, DC 20013-7127, USA

Steade Craigo — Historical Architect California Office of Historic Preservation, California Department of Parks and Recreation, PO Box 942896, Sacramento, CA 94296-0001, USA

Wayne Donaldson — Architect, Milford Wayne Donaldson and Associates, 530 Sixth Street, Suite 100, San Diego, CA 92101, USA

David G. Green — The Johnstone Centre, Charles Sturt University, PO Box 789, Albury NSW 2640, Australia

John Kariotis — Structural Engineer, Kariotis & Associates, 711 Mission Street, Suite D, South Pasadena, CA 91030, USA

Lisa Katchka — Office of General Counsel, Federal Emergency Management Agency, 500 C Street, SW, Room 840, Washington, DC 20472, USA

Alex Kimmelman — 1131 East Spring Street, Tucson, Arizona 85719, USA

Randolph Langenbach — Senior Analyst and Historic Building Specialist, Federal Emergency Management Agency, 500 C Street, SW, Room 713, Washington, DC 20007, USA

David W. Look — Chief, Cultural Resources Division, Pacific Regional Office, US National Park Service, 600 Harrison Street, San Francisco, CA 94104-1372, USA

Robert Mackensen — State Historic Building Safety Board, 1300 I Street, Suite 800, Sacramento, California 95814, USA

Stephen A. Mathison   Architectural Designer, Office of Archaeology and Historic Preservation, Department of Community Development, 111 21st Avenue, SW, Olympia, WA 98504-8343, USA

Ugo Morelli   Policy Manager, Earthquake Program, Federal Emergency Management Agency, 500 C Street, SW, Washington, DC 20472, USA

Eva Osborne .   Historic Preservation Architect, State Historic Preservation Office, 2704 Villa Prom, Shepherd Mall, Oklahoma City, OK 73107, USA

Daniel Shapiro   Shapiro Okino Hom & Associates, Structural Engineers, 303 2nd Street, Suite 305 South, San Francisco, California, CA 94107, USA

George O. Siekkinen Jr.   Historical Architect, National Trust for Historic Preservation, 1785 Massachusetts Avenue, NW, Washington, DC 20036, USA

Dirk H. R. Spennemann   Senior Lecturer, The Johnstone Centre, Charles Sturt University, PO Box 789, Albury NSW 2640, Australia

Diana Todd   Building and Fire Research Laboratory, National Institute of Standards & Technology, US Department of Commerce, Gaithersburg, Maryland, USA

Cherlyn Widell   State Historic Preservation Officer, California State Office of Historic Preservation, California Department of Parks & Recreation, PO Box 942896, Sacramento, CA 94296-0001, USA

Thomas A. Winter   Associate Architect, Northern Service Center, California Department of Parks and Recreation, 1725 23rd Street, Suite 200, Sacramento, CA 95816, USA

Index

☆ U.S. GOVERNMENT PRINTING OFFICE: 1998—685-765